HOCKEY

Publications International, Ltd.

ABOUT THE AUTHOR
James Duplacey has written numerous books on the history of hockey, including *Hockey Superstars: 1000 Point Players, Maple Leaf Magic,* and *Toronto Maple Leafs: Images of Glory.* He has served as curator of the Hockey Hall of Fame and Museum and managing editor of the *Official NHL Guide and Record Book.*

Contributing writers: James Duplacey, Marty Strasen

Louis Weber, CEO
Publications International, Ltd.
8140 Lehigh Avenue
Morton Grove, IL 60053

Permission is never granted for commercial purposes.

ISBN: 978-1-68022-545-7

Manufactured in China.

8 7 6 5 4 3 2 1

Library of Congress Control Number: 2016939494

CONTENTS

CHAPTER ONE
OPENING FACEOFF 4

CHAPTER TWO
GREATEST SHOW ON ICE 56

CHAPTER THREE
SLAP SHOTS 108

CHAPTER FOUR
POWER PLAYS 160

CHAPTER FIVE
LAST LINE OF DEFENSE 210

CHAPTER SIX
BACK OF THE NET 262

OPENING FACEOFF

"Every day is a great day for hockey."

—MARIO LEMIEUX

Wayne Gretzky
"The Great One"

A native of Brantford, Ontario, Wayne Gretzky spent his childhood years competing against older, stronger players. Yet he was always the best. At age 10 in the Brantford atom league, he scored 378 goals in 85 games. From then on, he captivated the hockey world.

With unparalleled instincts and graceful skating, Gretzky became a superstar despite his sparse build. In 1978, he signed a $1.75 million contract with the WHA's Indianapolis Racers. Sold to the Edmonton Oilers, he entered the NHL in 1979–80. That season Gretzky tied Marcel Dionne for the scoring lead (137 points), then proceeded to win the next seven scoring titles. In 1981–82, he amassed an NHL-record 92 goals and an unheard-of 212 points.

In 1983–84, Gretzky led the Oilers to their first Stanley Cup while pacing all playoff scorers (35 points in 19 games). Over the next four years, the Oilers won three more Cups. In nine brilliant seasons in Edmonton, Gretzky tallied 583 goals, 1,086 assists, and 1,669 points in 696 games. His truckload of awards included seven Art Ross Trophies, eight Hart Trophies, a pair of Conn Smythes, and the first of four Lady Byngs.

In 1988, Gretzky orchestrated his trade to Los Angeles, where he put hockey on the map as major entertainment. Moreover, he converted the Kings from doormats to playoff contenders. In 1993, he carried them all the way to the Stanley Cup Finals against Montreal. "The Great One" captured three more

> ## "I could hang a nickel in the net, and he'd hit it every time."
> —Floyd Whitney, part-time practice goalie for the Oilers in the 1980s

scoring titles—in 1990, '91, and '94.

On October 15, 1989, Gretzky notched his 1,851st point, passing his hero, Gordie Howe, to become the NHL's career scoring leader. On March 23, 1994, he tallied his 802nd goal to break Howe's record.

Traded to St. Louis late in 1995–96, Gretzky failed to "click" with right winger Brett Hull. As a free agent in the summer of 1996, he signed with the Rangers, where he reunited with ex-Oiler teammates Mark Messier and Jari Kurri for one last Cup chase. Gretzky, as executive director, helped Canada to a gold medal in the 2002 Olympics, then coached the Phoenix Coyotes for four seasons.

NHL STATISTICS

REGULAR SEASON					PLAYOFFS				
GP	G	A	PTS	PIM	GP	G	A	PTS	PIM
1,487	894	1,963	2,857	577	208	122	260	382	66

MAGICAL MOMENTS

PATRIARCH OF THE PADS

They called Lester Patrick "Silver Fox" for his silvery thatch of hair and his sly demeanor. The innovative coach, who built the New York Rangers into a championship-caliber club, also turned in one of the most amazing performances in Stanley Cup history. During Game 2 of the 1928 Finals against the Montreal Maroons, Rangers goalkeeper Lorne Chabot was hit in the head by a shot and was unable to continue. Coach Patrick, age 44, donned the pads and went between the pipes. Despite having no experience as a crease cop, the beetle-browed bench boss defeated Montreal 2–1 in overtime. The Broadway Blues went on to win their first Stanley Cup championship.

Robbed by a Lob

Before they bullied their way to the Stanley Cup winner's circle, the Philadelphia Flyers had to fight to merely make the playoffs. On two occasions, their postseason pursuit was halted by long bombs. In the final game of the 1969–70 season, a flip shot by Minnesota rookie Barry Gibbs bee-geed its way past Bernie Parent to fry the Flyers. Two years later, with mere ticks left on the clock, Sabres defenseman Gerry Meehan snapped a shot from center ice that somehow eluded the grasp of goalie Doug Favell and sent the Flyers to the golf course instead of the playoffs. Quipped Favell, "I lost it in the sun."

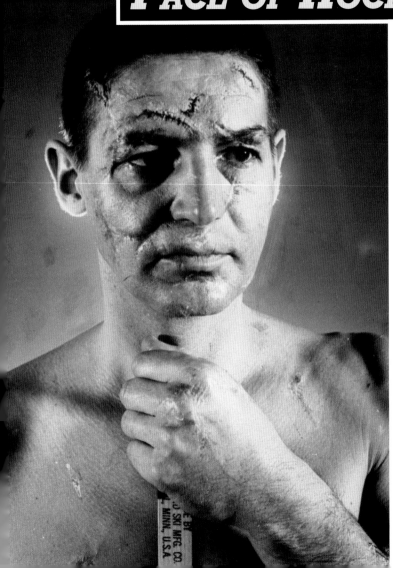

FACE OF HOCKEY

NHL goaltending legend Terry Sawchuk received 600 stitches during his career, including many on his face.

LUC ROBITAILLE

A natural goal-scorer who was largely ignored by NHL scouts as a junior, Luc Robitaille became the highest-scoring left winger in NHL history. The L.A. Kings' franchise leader in career goals (522), the nifty sharpshooter set NHL marks for most goals in a single season by a left winger (63) and most points in a season by a portsider (125). The Montreal native was named to the NHL's First All-Star Team on five occasions and retired with 668 career goals.

Put Me In, Coach

Ottawa Senators defender King Clancy was known as a feisty Irishman who used his sly sense of humor to talk himself out of trouble on the ice. During the 1923 Stanley Cup series against the Edmonton Eskimos, he talked himself into the hockey record books. When Ottawa goaltender Clint Benedict was flagged for tripping by the referee and forced to spend two minutes in the sin bin, Clancy volunteered to take his place between the pipes. Clancy, who had already skated as a defenseman, rover, and forward during the contest, became the only player in Stanley Cup history to play all six positions in the same game.

A brilliant tactician who displayed patience, courage, and fortitude, Bourque ranks second in NHL history with his 21 playoff appearances. His No. 77 was retired by both the Boston Bruins and the Colorado Avalanche.

Ray Bourque

"Always an All-Star"

Broke Wayne Gretzky's record by playing in the NHL All-Star Game for 19 consecutive seasons.

⬤ ⬤ ⬤

Won the Calder Trophy in 1979–80 and the King Clancy Trophy in 1991–92. Was named the NHL's top defenseman five times.

⬤ ⬤ ⬤

Holds NHL records for most goals (410), assists (1,169), and points (1,579) by a defenseman.

⬤ ⬤ ⬤

In 2001, he had the honor of being the first noncaptain to make the first lap around the ice with the Stanley Cup after finally winning the championship with Colorado.

NHL STATISTICS

REGULAR SEASON						PLAYOFFS				
GP	G	A	PTS	PIM		GP	G	A	PTS	PIM
1,612	410	1,169	1,579	1,141		214	41	139	180	171

VLADISLAV TRETIAK

The first Russian-trained player to be inducted into the Hockey Hall of Fame, Vladislav Tretiak compiled a minuscule 1.78 goals-against average in 98 international games. With Tretiak in goal, the Soviet national squad won the Olympic hockey title in 1972, 1976, and 1984. They also captured 10 world championships and nine European titles. In the 1981 Canada Cup, Tretiak was named the tournament MVP after posting an amazing 1.33 GAA over six games.

FAMOUS FIRSTS

1) Who was the first European-born captain to lead a team to the Stanley Cup Finals?

2) Who was the first defenseman to register 1,000 career points?

3) Who was the first player to have 14 consecutive 30-goal seasons?

4) Who was the first defenseman to record a hat trick in the Stanley Cup Finals?

5) Who was the first player to serve as captain on two Stanley Cup-winning teams?

6) Who was the first hockey player to appear on the cover of *Time* magazine?

Answers: 1) Daniel Alfredsson, 2) Denis Potvin, 3) Jaromir Jagr, 4) Eric Desjardins, 5) Mark Messier, 6) Lorne Chabot

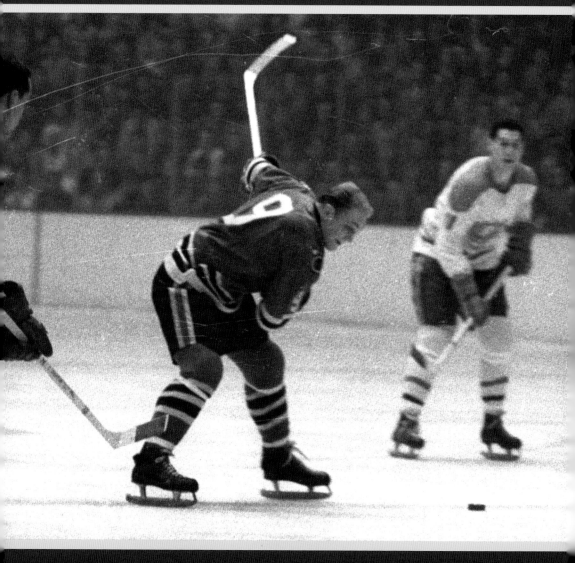

Thunderous Slapper

Known around the NHL as the "Golden Jet," Bobby Hull combined foot speed with powerful shooting to become the game's first player to score *50 goals twice*. His slap shot was once timed at 118.3 mph. On February 21, 1970, Hull, inventor of the curved stick blade, used his frightening slapper to beat Rangers goalie Ed Giacomin and became the NHL's *third-ever 500-goal scorer*, joining Rocket Richard and Gordie Howe.

★ ★ ★ ★ Hardest Shooters

Ray Bourque
Mike Bossy
Charlie Conacher
Bernie Geoffrion
Bobby Hull
Al Iafrate
Guy Lafleur
Al MacInnis
Frank Mahovlich
Fredrik Modin
Shea Weber

TALES OF THE
STANLEY CUP

THE MAN WHO STOLE THE STANLEY CUP

In the spring of 1962, the Chicago Blackhawks were on the verge of ending the Montreal Canadiens' grasp on Lord Stanley's mug. The Habs, who had carted home the hardware in five of the previous six seasons, were losing in the Cup semifinals to the Hawks when a loyal Canadiens fan, Ken Kilander, went and stole the trophy from its display case in the lobby of Chicago Stadium. Kilander, who was quickly apprehended, said that he had wanted to return the Cup to where he felt it belonged: Montreal.

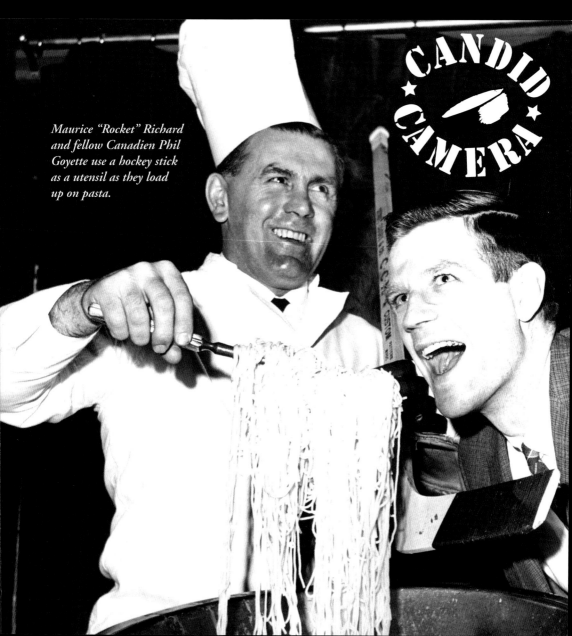

Maurice "Rocket" Richard and fellow Canadien Phil Goyette use a hockey stick as a utensil as they load up on pasta.

CANDID CAMERA

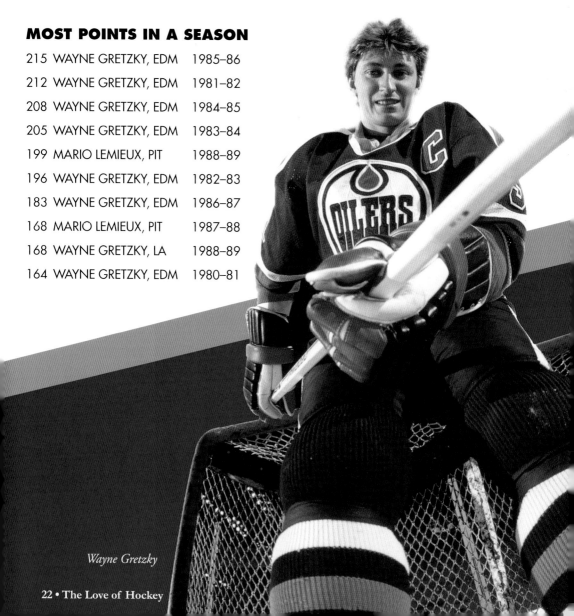

MOST POINTS IN A SEASON

215 WAYNE GRETZKY, EDM   1985–86
212 WAYNE GRETZKY, EDM   1981–82
208 WAYNE GRETZKY, EDM   1984–85
205 WAYNE GRETZKY, EDM   1983–84
199 MARIO LEMIEUX, PIT   1988–89
196 WAYNE GRETZKY, EDM   1982–83
183 WAYNE GRETZKY, EDM   1986–87
168 MARIO LEMIEUX, PIT   1987–88
168 WAYNE GRETZKY, LA   1988–89
164 WAYNE GRETZKY, EDM   1980–81

Wayne Gretzky

The Life of Riley

Many of the Canadian-born athletes who have fashioned a career in major-league baseball were also pretty fair hockey players who had to choose between the two sports. Jim Riley decided not to decide. He became the only man to play in both the major leagues and the NHL. A PCHA All-Star with the Seattle Metropolitans, Riley hung up the blades in 1924 and played two seasons of pro baseball, appearing in six games for the St. Louis Browns and Washington Senators. Riley returned to the ice in 1927, playing nine NHL games with the Detroit Cougars and the Chicago Black Hawks.

Bobby Orr

"Number 4"

Every once in a while a player comes along who revolutionizes his sport. In the late 1960s, a kid from Parry Sound, Ontario, turned the NHL on its ear with brilliant skating, unparalleled playmaking, and laser-beam shooting. The fact that he was a defenseman made his offensive feats all the more amazing.

Bobby Orr was an instant "impact player," scoring 13 goals and 41 points for the 1966–67 Bruins on his way to the Calder Trophy. He quickly became the NHL's most dangerous player and Boston's best weapon during its assault on the Stanley Cup. In 1967–68, while battling a knee injury, he notched 31 points in 46 games and earned his first of eight straight Norris Trophies. In 1969–70, he won the Art Ross Trophy with 120 points, becoming the first back-liner ever to win a scoring title. He added the Hart Trophy as MVP and, at age 22, was called the greatest defenseman ever.

In 1969–70, Orr and Phil Esposito led the Big, Bad Bruins to the Finals against St. Louis. Just 40 seconds into overtime in Game 4, Orr beat goalie Glenn Hall—leaping through the air with his stick held high—to end Boston's 29-year Stanley Cup drought. Orr's winning goal and 20 playoff points earned him the Conn Smythe Trophy.

In 1970–71, Orr logged 102 assists—smashing the league record for helpers by a defenseman—and finished second in points (139) to Esposito (152). Orr

> ## "He's the only player I've ever seen who can operate at top speed—wide-open, breakneck speed—and still execute all the fundamentals of the game."
>
> —Bruins coach Harry Sinden on Bobby Orr, *Time* magazine, January 5, 1968

took home his fourth Norris Trophy and his second Hart Trophy. A year later, he finished second in points (117) and won his fifth Norris and third Hart. In the playoffs, his 19 assists topped the charts as Boston roared to its second Stanley Cup in three years. Orr tied Esposito in playoff points (24) and scored his second Cup-clinching goal, in Game 6 versus the Rangers, to win another Conn Smythe Trophy.

Knee injuries plagued Orr and ultimately cut his career short. He won his second Art Ross with 135 points in 1974–75, his last full season in the NHL.

NHL STATISTICS

REGULAR SEASON					PLAYOFFS				
GP	G	A	PTS	PIM	GP	G	A	PTS	PIM
657	270	645	915	953	74	26	66	92	92

CAROLINA ON MY MIND

When the Hartford Whalers relocated to Carolina prior to the 1997–98 season, the beleaguered franchise carried with it a string of exasperating postseason failures. In 2001–02, the replanted and renamed Carolina Hurricanes became the last WHA-era team to reach the Stanley Cup Finals, and it lost in five games to the Detroit Red Wings. In 2005–06, the Hurricanes returned to the championship round. Bolstered by the heroics of rookie goaltender Cam Ward and the gritty determination of captain Rod Brind'Amour, the 'Canes outlasted the stubborn Edmonton Oilers in seven grueling games to deliver the Stanley Cup to the heartland of NASCAR.

Rod Brind'Amour

A Goalie Trifecta

On October 22, 2002, Lexington Men O'War netminder Mike Smith became the first goaltender in hockey history to record a "goalie trifecta." Smith collected his first professional win, first professional shutout, and first professional goal in the same game. With the War men leading the ECHL's Dayton Bombers 1—0 late in the third period, Smith perfectly placed a clearing attempt into the vacated Dayton cage to secure Lexington's 2—0 victory. Four years later, Smith repeated two parts of the trifecta in his NHL debut with Dallas, when he whitewashed the Phoenix Coyotes 2—0 on October 21, 2006.

GNASH

Saber-toothed and superbly coordinated, Gnash is the official mascot of the Nashville Predators. The blue-colored cat was one of the first NHL mascots to use precisely orchestrated stunts, such as rappelling through the rafters, to entertain the zany zealots in the country music capital of the USA.

THE CASH BOX
ON CARLTON

Dreamed up by Conn Smythe and built during the
height of the Great Depression by workmen who
agreed to take part of their payment in stocks,
Maple Leaf Gardens made its owners richer than
they could ever have imagined. With a Stanley
Cup championship in its first season (1931–32)
and 10 more titles from 1942 to 1967, the Maple
Leafs and their arena became Canadian institu-
tions. Even when the championships ceased, the
turnstiles kept spinning, with sellout crowds for
every game from 1946 to '99.

FANTASTIC FANS

A New Jersey Devils fan enjoys the pre-game party outside the Continental Airlines Arena prior to a playoff game against the Rangers on April 24, 2006.

"Half of this game is mental, **the other half is being mental.**"

—Jim McKenny,
former NHL defenseman

STANLEY CUP CLASSICS

SEVEN GAMES AND BEYOND

The Red Wings entered the 1950 Stanley Cup Finals without Gordie Howe. In the previous series, against Toronto, he suffered a head injury so serious that he required two delicate brain operations. Despite playing all their games on the road because the circus was occupying Madison Square Garden, the Rangers had the Red Wings on the ropes in the 1950 Stanley Cup Finals. New York took a 3–2 series lead after Don "Bones" Raleigh scored overtime winners in back-to-back games. But Detroit rallied to force the series to seven games and beyond. Finally, at 8:31 of the second overtime period, Pete Babando flipped a shot past NHL MVP Chuck Rayner to give Detroit a victory in the first Game 7 in Stanley Cup Finals history to go into overtime.

Gordie Howe leaving on a stretcher

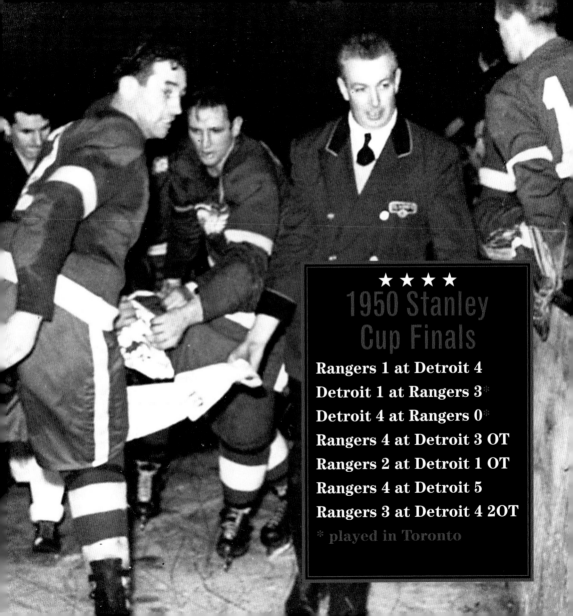

★ ★ ★ ★
1950 Stanley Cup Finals

Rangers 1 at Detroit 4
Detroit 1 at Rangers 3*
Detroit 4 at Rangers 0*
Rangers 4 at Detroit 3 OT
Rangers 2 at Detroit 1 OT
Rangers 4 at Detroit 5
Rangers 3 at Detroit 4 2OT

* played in Toronto

DOMINIK HASEK

Dominik "The Dominator" Hasek revolutionized goaltending with his contortionist style of play. For Buffalo in 1996–97, he became the first goalie to win the Hart Trophy in 35 years, then repeated as league MVP a year later. Hasek holds the Sabres' all-time records for wins (234) and shutouts (55). A six-time winner of the Vezina Trophy, Hasek guided the Red Wings into the Stanley Cup winner's circle in 2001–02.

A Carolina fan personifies the "Cinderella" Hurricanes during the third game of the 2002 Stanley Cup Finals. After winning a modest 35 games during the season, the 'Canes stormed to the Finals to face the mighty Wings. For this Cinderella team, the clock struck midnight literally during a Game 3 triple-overtime loss and figuratively with Detroit's series-clinching triumph in Game 5.

Bryan Trottier

"The Leader"

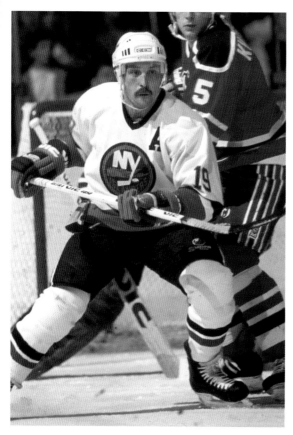

As the Islanders constructed their dynasty a generation ago, center Bryan Trottier emerged as the team's heart and soul. Despite such competition as Bobby Clarke and Wayne Gretzky, Trottier was considered the best two-way pivot in the game during much of his 18-year career.

Tough as nails and blessed with the grace of a natural playmaker, Trottier debuted with the Isles in 1975–76 and won the Calder Trophy with 95 points. Two years later, in 1977–78, he paced the Isles in scoring with 123 points (including 46 goals) and made the NHL First All-Star Team. Teamed with rugged Clark Gillies to the left and sniper Mike Bossy to the right, Trottier soared to new heights, winning the 1979 scoring title with 134 points, including a league-high 87 assists. Trottier also won the Hart Trophy as MVP. Favored to win the last Cup of the '70s, Trottier and the Islanders endured the last of their growing pains when they were upset by the Rangers in the 1979 Cup semifinals. But the NHL was put on notice: The Islanders are coming!

In 1979–80, Trottier took the Isles to hallowed ground. After enjoying his third of six 100-point seasons, he led all playoff scorers with 12 goals and 29 points. The Isles won their first Stanley Cup on a Game 6 sudden-death OT goal from Bobby Nystrom and began an era of eminence that would place them among the great dynasties of all

time. Voted the Conn Smythe Trophy as playoff MVP, Trottier entered his salad days as a team leader, a role in which he was unrivaled.

While Trottier had given up hope of winning another scoring title (due to Gretzky's emergence), his effectiveness at the helm continued. In 1981–82, he led all playoff scorers with 29 points, and the Isles hoisted their third straight Cup. Trottier won his fourth Stanley Cup title in 1983 before injuries and age took their final toll.

After 15 years with the Isles, Trottier signed with Pittsburgh in 1990–91. In a supporting role, he played three years, taught the young Pens how to win, and added two more Stanley Cups to his extraordinary résumé.

NHL STATISTICS

REGULAR SEASON					PLAYOFFS				
GP	G	A	PTS	PIM	GP	G	A	PTS	PIM
1,279	524	901	1,425	912	221	71	113	184	277

Hall of Fame Treasures

The skates of Cy Denneny (above) date back to the early days of the NHL. The Ottawa Senators legend finished second in the league in scoring in 1917–18—the NHL's inaugural campaign—and won the scoring title in 1923–24. The skates on the right belonged to Wayne Gretzky—the first he ever wore.

MOST CAREER POINTS

WAYNE GRETZKY	2,857
MARK MESSIER	1,887
JAROMIR JAGR	1,868
GORDIE HOWE	1,850
RON FRANCIS	1,798
MARCEL DIONNE	1,771
STEVE YZERMAN	1,755
MARIO LEMIEUX	1,723
JOE SAKIC	1,641
PHIL ESPOSITO	1,590

Mark Messier

Eight Arms to Hold You

On April 15, 1952, two zany, hockey-loving brothers from Detroit began what would become one of hockey's most famous traditions. That evening, Jerry and Pete Cusimano, who owned a fish store in Motown, smuggled an octopus into the Olympia. They chose the much-maligned mollusk because its eight arms represented the number of wins necessary to capture Lord Stanley's coveted mug. When Gordie Howe scored the first goal of the game that evening, one of the brothers unleashed the sea serpent, beginning an octopus parade that has continued to this day—despite the NHL's attempts to curtail the fishy spectacle.

New York, New York

Nothing incites more passion than a good old-fashioned crosstown rivalry. And when it comes to bitter acrimony, savage sarcasm, and **demented denizens,** an Islanders-Rangers contest stands alone. Regardless of positioning in the standings or quality of the season-by-season competition, each tussle is a tempest in a boiling teapot. From the Islanders' first overtime victory over the Broadway Blues in the 1975 playoffs to the cascading chorus of "Potvin sucks" that rocks the Madison Square madhouse, this attraction has tradition, *vitality, and attitude.*

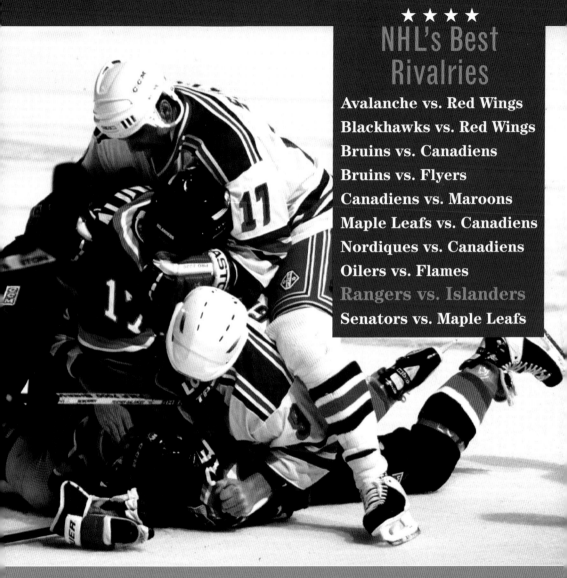

Avalanche vs. Red Wings

Blackhawks vs. Red Wings

Bruins vs. Canadiens

Bruins vs. Flyers

Canadiens vs. Maroons

Maple Leafs vs. Canadiens

Nordiques vs. Canadiens

Oilers vs. Flames

Rangers vs. Islanders

Senators vs. Maple Leafs

MAGICAL MOMENTS

HENDERSON'S HEROICS

The 1972 Summit Series between Canada and the Soviet Union was the first opportunity for the NHL's best players to match their skills against the most dominant hockey power overseas—the Soviet national team. Most scribes predicted easy victories for Canada, but when the final game entered its last minute, the teams were all square in the series (3–3–1) and tied 5–5 in the match. With only 34 ticks remaining, Team Canada forward Paul Henderson—who already had scored the winning goal in the previous two games—corralled a rebound near the Soviet cage and slipped the series-winning shot under Russian goalie Vladislav Tretiak.

Phil Esposito, Paul Henderson,
Yvon Cournoyer (left to right)

What's My Line?

This trio of brothers played together on the same Black Hawks line in 1942–43. The center, Max, would go on to win the 1945–46 Hart Trophy. Doug (*right*) toiled from 1939 to '52 in the Windy City. Reggie (*left*), the oldest of the brothers, played in 11 NHL games. Who were they?

Answer: The Bentleys

GUYLE FIELDER

A brilliant playmaker who was renowned for his ability to feather a picture-perfect pass through a maze of sticks and legs, Guyle Fielder was the first player in hockey history to record 2,000 career points. A native of Potlatch, Idaho, Fielder led the WHL in assists 12 times and was adorned as the rookie of the year in three different leagues. A six-time WHL MVP in the 1950s and '60s, Fielder collected at least 100 points in six different seasons.

Brett Hull

"The Golden Brett"

Scored 741 career goals, the third highest total in NHL history upon his retirement, and collected 1,391 points during his 20-year NHL career.

● ● ●

Won the Lady Byng Trophy in 1989–90 and the Hart Trophy as league MVP in 1990–91, the year he scored 86 goals for St. Louis.

● ● ●

Was named to the NHL First All-Star Team three straight years, from 1989–90 to 1991–92, scoring more than 70 goals in each of those seasons.

NHL STATISTICS

REGULAR SEASON					PLAYOFFS				
GP	G	A	PTS	PIM	GP	G	A	PTS	PIM
1,269	741	650	1,391	458	202	103	87	190	73

Brett and his father, Bobby Hull, are the only father-son combination to win the Hart Trophy as league MVP and score more than 600 goals apiece. Brett scored the Stanley Cup-winning goal for Dallas in 1999.

"**Red's got every move in the book** and then some. He's big. **He skates like an express train**, and he shoots as hard as anyone in the league, including Bobby Hull."

—Glenn Hall on the St. Louis Blues' Red Berenson, the first expansion-team superstar

From the Classroom to the Dressing Room

In the early 1980s, four exceptional American players went directly from high school to the NHL, becoming the first and last players to do so. Bobby Carpenter, the Washington Capitals' top pick in the 1981 draft, was the first American-born player to score 50 goals in a season. Phil Housley, who retired in 2003 as the highest-scoring U.S.-born player in NHL history, joined the Buffalo Sabres directly from South St. Paul High School in 1982. In 1983–84, teammate Tom Barrasso became the first NHL goalie to win the Calder and Vezina trophies a year after playing high school hockey. Brian Lawton, the first American player to be chosen first overall in the NHL draft, began his career with Minnesota in 1983–84.

BERNIE PARENT

The backbone backstop of the Broadway Bullies, Bernie Parent guided the Philadelphia Flyers to back-to-back Stanley Cup championships in 1974 and '75. A stand-up goalie with a rapier-quick glove, Parent won the goaltending triple crown by leading all NHL crease cops in wins, shutouts, and GAA in 1973–74 and 1974–75. He also became the first player to win back-to-back Conn Smythe Trophies as playoff MVP.

The Net Cam

Buffalo goalie Ryan Miller and teammate Teppo Numminen watch a shot by Ottawa's Jason Spezza sail to the back of the net during Game 3 of the 2006 Eastern Conference semifinals. The Sabres won the contest 3–2 in overtime and took the series in five games.

CHAPTER TWO

GREATEST SHOW ON ICE

"They are just grown-up kids who have learned on the frozen creek or flooded corner lot that hockey is the greatest thrill of all."

—LESTER PATRICK

Joe Sakic

"Super Joe"

Collected at least 100 points six times, including the 2006–07 season, when he became the second oldest player (37) in NHL history to hit the century mark.

● ● ●

Won the Conn Smythe Trophy (1995–96), the Hart Trophy (2000–01), and the Lady Byng Trophy (2000–01).

● ● ●

Established an NHL record with six game-winning goals during the 1996 playoffs. Scored 18 playoff goals in 1996, the second highest total in league history.

● ● ●

Was named tournament MVP of the 2002 Olympic Games as well as MVP of the 2004 NHL All-Star Game.

NHL STATISTICS

REGULAR SEASON						PLAYOFFS				
GP	G	A	PTS	PIM		GP	G	A	PTS	PIM
1,378	625	1,016	1,641	614		172	84	104	188	78

CYCLONE TAYLOR

Frederick Wellington Taylor was known as "Cyclone" during his playing career because of his explosive speed and ability to dart between defenders to find an open lane to the net. Taylor played on a pair of Stanley Cup-winning teams and scored 205 goals over his illustrious 21-year career (1902–23). He won five scoring titles in the Pacific Coast Hockey Association, and he was awarded the Order of the British Empire by King George VI for his outstanding service during World War II.

What's My Line?

This Rangers trio of the late 1960s and early '70s featured Jean Ratelle (*right*) at center, Rod Gilbert (*middle*) on right wing, and Vic Hadfield (*left*) on the port side. The high-scoring unit wasn't broken up until 1975, when Ratelle was dealt to Boston in the Phil Esposito blockbuster trade. What was the name of this legendary line?

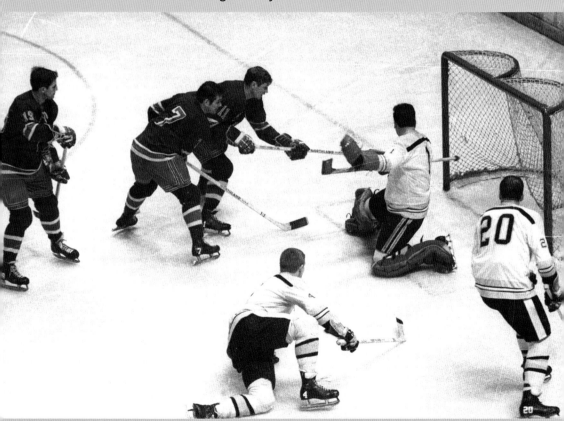

Answer: Goal-a-Game Line (or GAG Line)

THE JET PASSES THE ROCKET

With his wavy blond locks, sculptured physique, and blistering slap shot, Bobby Hull electrified fans in NHL arenas throughout the 1960s. After tying Maurice Richard's record of 50 goals in a season in only his fifth NHL campaign, it seemed just a matter of time before the "Jet" roared past the "Rocket." In a game against the Rangers on March 12, 1966, Hull finally erased Richard's mark from the record books. With just over five minutes remaining in the first stanza, he crossed over the blue line, slammed on the brakes, and blazed a laser past Cesare Maniago. That patented blast earned the "Golden One" a seven-minute standing ovation and a place in NHL lore.

The Grate One

During his career, Claude Lemieux was known by a litany of nicknames, most of them too vulgar to be printed on these pages. Noted for his on-ice nastiness, antagonistic attitude, and yammering yapping, Lemieux also forged a reputation as a winner. As a rookie with only 19 NHL games under his belt, he scored 10 postseason goals to help the Montreal Canadiens capture the Stanley Cup in 1986. Impressively, he won three more Cup titles—New Jersey in 1995, Colorado in 1996, and the Devils again in 2000. He is one of just nine players to win Cups with three different teams.

Howie Morenz

"The Stratford Streak"

One of the largest crowds ever to fill the Montreal Forum didn't come to watch a hockey game but to pay respects to a hero. In March 1937, thousands of fans passed the coffin of Howie Morenz as he lay in state at center ice. Morenz, who had died suddenly at 34 while recovering in the hospital from hockey injuries, was arguably the greatest player ever to wear the *bleu, blanc, et rouge* of *Les Habs*.

As a rookie in 1923–24, Morenz led Montreal to its first Stanley Cup when the Habs won a best-of-three set against Calgary of the WCHL. Morenz ripped a hat trick in Game 1 (a 6–1 rout), then scored the opening goal, the winner, in a 3–0 Cup-clinching victory in Game 2.

With explosive skating speed that earned him the nickname "The Stratford Streak" (after his hometown in Ontario), Morenz began to dominate in 1927–28, when he led the NHL in goals (33) and won his first Art Ross Trophy with 51 points. He also won the Hart Trophy as MVP. Playing on a line with Aurel Joliat and Art Gagne (and later Johnny "Black Cat" Gagnon), Morenz became one of the NHL's top snipers. In 1929–30, he scored a career-high 40 goals and led the Canadiens over the Boston Bruins in the Stanley Cup Finals. He scored the Cup-winning goal late in the second period of Game 2, a nail-biting 4–3 conquest.

In 1930–31, Morenz copped his second Art Ross Trophy (28 goals, 51 points) and second Hart Trophy. In the playoffs, he was quiet until the last game of the Finals against Chicago. With Montreal holding a 1–0 lead late in the game, Morenz beat Charlie Gardiner for his only goal of the series, ensuring Montreal's victory.

Morenz won his last Hart Trophy in 1931–32, after which his scoring began to fade. In 1934–35, he was traded to Chicago, where he stayed less than two years before playing briefly with the Rangers. He rejoined the Habs in 1936–37, as a shadow of his former self, then suffered a badly broken leg during the campaign. While hospitalized, he suffered a fatal heart attack. All of Canada mourned the fallen hero.

> "The rink was jammed to the rafters with fans standing motionless with heads bared."
>
> —Journalist Andy O'Brien, describing the funeral service for Morenz at the Montreal Forum

NHL STATISTICS

REGULAR SEASON				
GP	G	A	PTS	PIM
550	270	197	467	531

YOUPPI

The first switch-hitting mascot in major-league sports history, Youppi originally yucked it up with baseball's Montreal Expos. When the franchise relocated to Washington, D.C., the Canadiens adopted the character as the first mascot in team annals. Youppi officially took over the cheerleading duties for *Les Glorieux* on September 16, 2005.

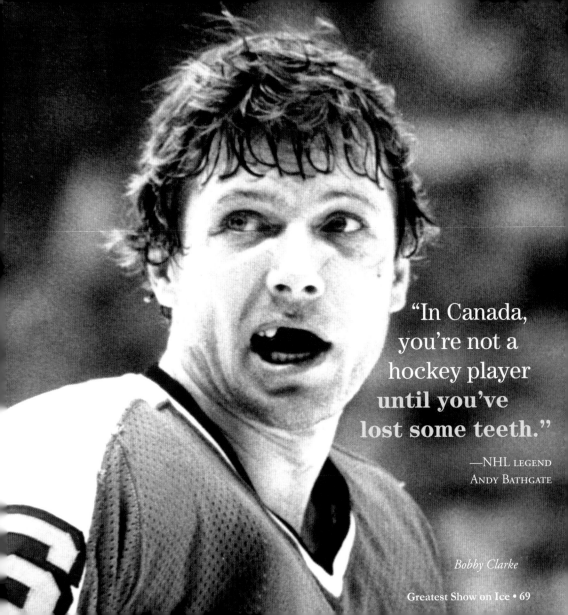

"In Canada, you're not a hockey player until you've lost some teeth."

—NHL LEGEND ANDY BATHGATE

Bobby Clarke

THE CANADIEN CATHEDRAL

From its opening in 1924 to its emotional farewell on March 11, 1996, the Montreal Forum was home to a seemingly endless succession of brilliant stars and championship teams. From Howie Morenz to Maurice Richard to Guy Lafleur to Patrick Roy, the Canadiens ruled hockey with Gallic flair, winning more Stanley Cup titles than any team in history. Whether in the original modest facility of 9,300 seats or in the 18,000-seat refurbished Forum (post-1968), only one visiting team was ever able to beat the Canadiens for the Stanley Cup on the Forum's fabled ice.

PETER FORSBERG

The first European-trained player to perfect the hard-checking, bone-bruising North American style of hockey, Peter Forsberg was as comfortable battling in the corners as he was snapping home loose pucks from a scrum at the lip of the crease. In 1993, Forsberg set an IIHF record with 31 points in only seven games during the World Junior Hockey championships. The Swedish sensation led Colorado to two Stanley Cups and won the Hart and Art Ross trophies in 2002–03.

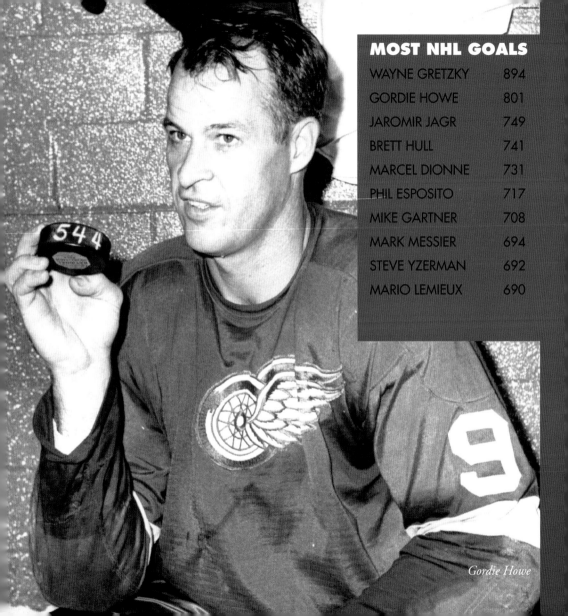

MOST NHL GOALS

WAYNE GRETZKY	894
GORDIE HOWE	801
JAROMIR JAGR	749
BRETT HULL	741
MARCEL DIONNE	731
PHIL ESPOSITO	717
MIKE GARTNER	708
MARK MESSIER	694
STEVE YZERMAN	692
MARIO LEMIEUX	690

Gordie Howe

Mike Bossy

"The Boss"

Blessed with soft hands, a smooth-skating style, and a
rapid-fire release, Bossy tweaked the twine at least
50 times in each of his first nine seasons in the NHL.

● ● ●

Became in 1980–81 only the second player in NHL history
to score 50 goals in 50 games, tying Maurice Richard's
vaunted mark.

● ● ●

Helped lead the New York Islanders to four consecutive
Stanley Cup titles (1980–81 to 1983–84).

● ● ●

Became the first player to score at least 17 playoff goals
in three consecutive postseason campaigns.

NHL STATISTICS

REGULAR SEASON					PLAYOFFS				
GP	G	A	PTS	PIM	GP	G	A	PTS	PIM
752	573	533	1,126	210	129	85	75	160	38

"Nobody sets out to break records. You just play, you score, and they happen. But the 50-in-50, that's one I want. Having my name next to Richard would not be too shabby."

—Mike Bossy, *Time*, February 2, 1981

The Russian Revolution

Near the conclusion of the 1988—89 season, an unheralded and virtually unknown player made his NHL debut and completely changed the complexion of the league forever. Sergei Priakin, a 12th-round draft selection of Calgary, became the first Russian-born and -trained player to cross the pond and play in the NHL with the full approval of the Soviet Ice Hockey Federation. Within weeks of Priakin's NHL debut, three of the greatest players in Russian hockey history signed contracts with NHL teams. Calgary inked Sergei Makarov, New Jersey landed Slava Fetisov, and Vancouver signed Igor Larionov.

Sergei Makarov

FANTASTIC FANS

This Red Wings fan brought a cup to the Joe for Game 5 of the 2002 Western Conference finals against the Avalanche. Colorado won 2–1 in overtime, but Detroit weathered the Avalanche and then the Hurricanes to win the real Stanley Cup.

Iron Man

Although he toiled for 15 seasons as a professional goaltender, Robbie Irons's NHL career lasted only three minutes—but it was a momentous 180 seconds. Promoted to St. Louis, Irons was on the bench as the Blues battled the Rangers on November 13, 1968. It was the first time that Blues goalie Glenn Hall wore a mask during a game and the only time in his long career that he received a game misconduct. Hall took exception to a St. Louis penalty and challenged the referee to reverse the call with some unsavory language. That earned Hall the thumb and Irons the chance. Irons patrolled the crease until Jacques Plante, who scrambled out of the stands and into the pads, replaced him. Irons never played in the NHL again.

Toeing the Line

Throughout the latter half of the 1990s, the NHL employed a rule regarding enemy encampment in the goaltender's crease. No part of a player's anatomy or equipment was permitted in the crease area or even on the line. Although the edict was introduced to protect the netminder, the legislation was so strictly enforced that even empty-net goals were called off if a player's stick or skate dipped into the crease. After Dallas winger Brett Hull's Stanley Cup-winning goal against Buffalo in 1999 was allowed to stand, even though the tip of his toe was touching the lip of the crease, the league had no other option but to relax the restrictions.

Hull's controversial goal

STANLEY CUP CLASSICS

SEVENTH HEAVEN

The Rangers had not won the Stanley Cup since 1940, which rival fans of the Islanders loved to taunt them about. But after Mark Messier led the Rangers to a dramatic triumph over the New Jersey Devils in the 1994 Eastern Conference finals, the Rangers raced out to a three-games-to-one lead in their Stanley Cup series against Vancouver. The Canucks spoiled plans for a victory party with a win in Game 5, then forced the series to the limit with another triumph in Game 6. Finally, the Rangers ended their 54-year drought with a spine-chilling 3–2 victory. Declared a fan's banner in the Garden: "Now I Can Die in Peace."

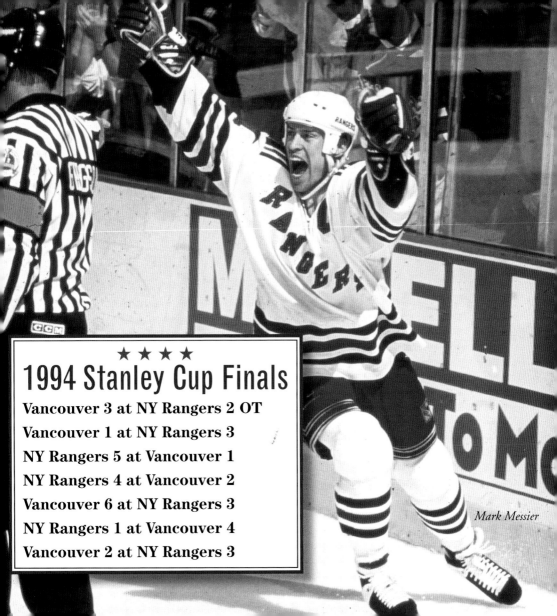

★ ★ ★ ★
1994 Stanley Cup Finals
Vancouver 3 at NY Rangers 2 OT

Vancouver 1 at NY Rangers 3

NY Rangers 5 at Vancouver 1

NY Rangers 4 at Vancouver 2

Vancouver 6 at NY Rangers 3

NY Rangers 1 at Vancouver 4

Vancouver 2 at NY Rangers 3

Mark Messier

These two young fans, attending a World Cup of Hockey game in Montreal on September 1, 2004, suggest a way to keep the NHL in business. Alas, no man or child suited up in 2004–05 due to a labor dispute. The entire NHL season was canceled.

PAVEL BURE

Nicknamed the "Russian Rocket," Pavel Bure had the ability to lift fans out of their seats with his breathtaking speed, delicious dexterity, and quick, soft hands. The first Vancouver player to score 60 goals in back-to-back seasons (1992–93 and 1993–94), Bure twice led the league in goals with the Florida Panthers (58 in 1999–2000 and 59 the following year).

Jean Beliveau

"Gentleman Jean"

Served as distinguished captain of the Canadiens
for 10 of his 20 NHL seasons.

● ● ●

Won 10 Stanley Cup titles with Montreal and, in 1964,
became the first winner of the Conn Smythe Trophy as
playoff MVP.

● ● ●

Won two Hart Trophies as NHL MVP and led the league in
scoring in 1955–56 (88 points). Was selected to the NHL
First All-Star Team six times.

● ● ●

Retired as Montreal's all-time leading scorer in
both the regular season and the playoffs.

NHL STATISTICS

REGULAR SEASON					PLAYOFFS				
GP	G	A	PTS	PIM	GP	G	A	PTS	PIM
1,125	507	712	1,219	1,029	162	79	97	176	211

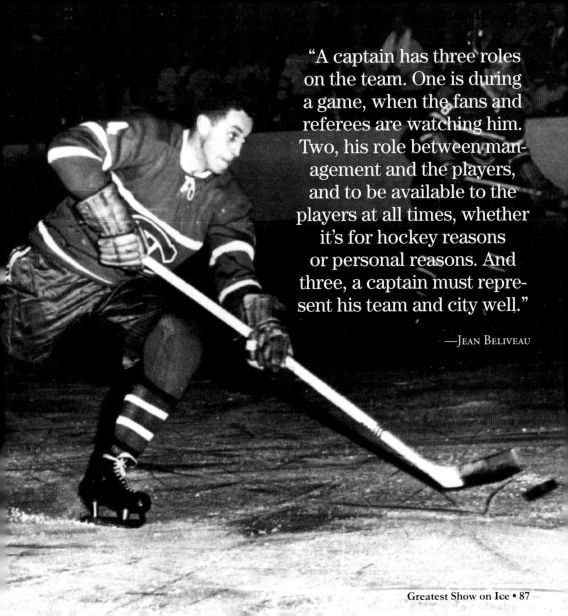

"A captain has three roles on the team. One is during a game, when the fans and referees are watching him. Two, his role between management and the players, and to be available to the players at all times, whether it's for hockey reasons or personal reasons. And three, a captain must represent his team and city well."

—Jean Beliveau

LONELY ONLY

1) Who was the only player to serve as captain of two different Stanley Cup-winning teams?

2) Who was the only goalie to win two or more Stanley Cup championships with two or more teams?

3) Who was the only athlete to play major-league baseball and NHL hockey?

4) Who was the only NHL coach to serve as a major-league baseball umpire?

5) Who was the only player in NHL history to score a goal on his only NHL shot?

6) Who was the only goalie to win rookie of the year honors in three different pro leagues?

Answers: 1) Mark Messier, 2) Patrick Roy, 3) Jim Riley, 4) Bill Stewart, 5) Chris McRae, 6) Terry Sawchuk

HALL OF FAME TREASURES

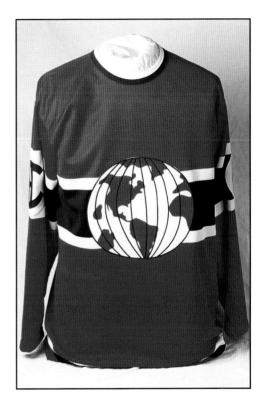

Standout goalie Hap Holmes wore this jersey with the PCHA's Seattle Metropolitans, who in 1917 became the first NHL team to win the Stanley Cup.

After winning the Stanley Cup in 1924, the Montreal Canadiens adopted this sweater design the following season, signifying that they were world champs.

The Delivery Boy – The media spotlight has shone on Sidney Crosby ever since he was 10, when he amassed 280 points for his hometown team in Cole Harbour, Nova Scotia. Saddled with enormous expectations, "Sid the Kid" has delivered on the promise with quiet grace and outrageous talent. Crosby rose to prominence during his sophomore season. At age 19 in 2006–07, he became the youngest player ever to win an NHL scoring title (120 points) and only the seventh player to win the Hart, Art Ross, and Lester Pearson trophies in the same season. Crosby led the Penguins to a 2009 Stanley Cup victory, becoming the youngest player (21) to captain a team to the Cup since 1895.

Sidney Crosby (left)
with Ryan Malone

PAUL COFFEY

The only NHL defenseman to score at least 40 goals in a season twice in his career, Paul Coffey was an explosive skater who helped lead Edmonton to three Stanley Cup championships. Coffey, who holds the NHL record for goals in a season by a blueliner with 48, is the only defenseman to go nine years between Norris Trophy wins (1986, 1995). He toiled for nine NHL teams in his 21-year, Hall of Fame career.

In the fall of 1949, beefy Maple Leafs goalie Turk Broda responded to manager Conn Smythe's demand that he lose some weight. The 35-year-old Broda won what the press called the "Battle of the Bulge" and proceeded to have his best season in years, posting a 2.45 GAA.

CANDID CAMERA

TOLEDO

NO SPRINGS - HONEST WEIGHT

Beef
Only about 55 per cent of the live weight is meat. The balance is by-products or waste.

Club Steak

Sirloin Steak

Porterhouse Steak

Slower cooking cuts are economical and delicious.

Round

Round Steak

Rolled Rib Roast

Loin

Rib

Standing Rib Roast

Chuck

Rump Roast

Side of Beef

Flank Steak

Quick cooking steaks and roasts comprise only 26 per cent. of a side of beef.

Beef Cuts
1	Round	24%
2	Loin	17%
3	Rib	9%
4	Flank	4%
5	Chuck or shoulder	26%
6	Plate	12%
7	Shank	4%
8	Suet	4%
		100%

Brisket
Corned Beef

Compli...
of
SWIFT & CO...

Steve Yzerman

"Stevie Wonder"

A championship-caliber tennis player in his youth, Steve Yzerman tossed the racquet aside when he realized he could make more money whacking a puck. The court's loss was the rink's gain. When Yzerman applied his remarkable talent to the ice surface, he revived a dismal franchise and helped Motown become Hockeytown USA.

Following a brief but promising junior career with the Peterborough Petes of the OHL, Yzerman was drafted fourth overall by the Red Wings. In his first NHL campaign (1983–84), he set club records for goals (39) and points (87) by a freshman and became, at age 18, the youngest participant ever in the NHL All-Star Game. When Yzerman was named captain of the club in 1986, he became the youngest player in NHL history to don the "C."

Employing his superior skills and uncanny hockey instincts, Yzerman collected at least 100 points in six consecutive seasons from 1987–88 to 1992–93, including a career-high 155 points in 1988–89. That year, he was awarded the Lester Pearson Trophy as the best player in the league, as voted by his on-ice brethren.

Although the Red Wings continued to prosper under his guidance, the team was unable to translate regular-season success into postseason prosperity. To help his team scale hockey's most difficult plateau, Yzerman resorted to the lessons he had learned during the 1987 Canada Cup competition, when he was asked to dedicate his game to prevention as much as production. Playing an industrious two-way role, Yzerman provided quiet leadership and untiring work ethic to propel the Wings to the Stanley Cup title in 1997 and 1998.

Yzerman continued to produce on the ice, and although his offensive numbers never reached the lofty heights he had achieved in the late 1980s, his club became the model for NHL consistency. The Wings continuously finished near the top rung of the yearly standings and returned the Stanley Cup to Motown in 2002. A string of injuries and the nagging sands of time eventually brought Yzerman's career to a close in 2006.

After hanging up the blades, Yzerman became general manager of Canada's entry in the 2007 World Hockey Championships. Despite a hastily constructed lineup, the team went undefeated.

NHL STATISTICS

REGULAR SEASON					PLAYOFFS				
GP	G	A	PTS	PIM	GP	G	A	PTS	PIM
1,514	692	1,063	1,755	924	196	70	115	185	84

MIRACLE ON ICE

On February 22, 1980, the U.S. Olympic hockey team stunned the world by defeating the Soviet national team 4–3 in the medal round of the 1980 Olympic hockey tournament, staged in Lake Placid, New York. Hastily assembled by coach Herb Brooks (the last player cut from the gold medal-winning 1960 Olympic team), the American collection of collegiate players had lost to the Russians 10–3 in a warmup tilt only days before the start of the Olympics. The winning marker was scored by team captain Mike Eruzione, one of the few players on the club who did not translate his Olympic success into an NHL paycheck. The Americans went on to defeat Finland 4–2 to capture the gold medal.

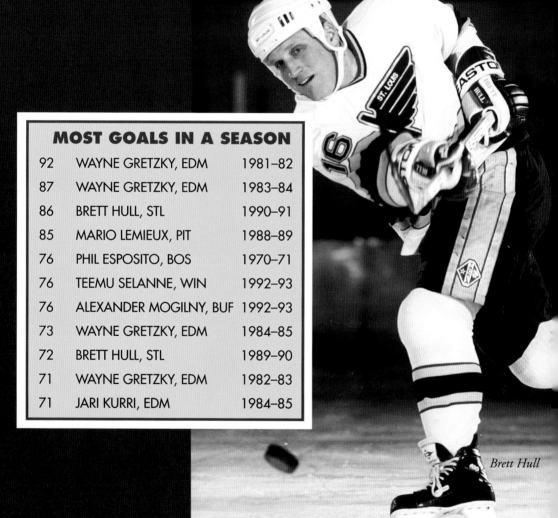

MOST GOALS IN A SEASON

92	WAYNE GRETZKY, EDM	1981–82
87	WAYNE GRETZKY, EDM	1983–84
86	BRETT HULL, STL	1990–91
85	MARIO LEMIEUX, PIT	1988–89
76	PHIL ESPOSITO, BOS	1970–71
76	TEEMU SELANNE, WIN	1992–93
76	ALEXANDER MOGILNY, BUF	1992–93
73	WAYNE GRETZKY, EDM	1984–85
72	BRETT HULL, STL	1989–90
71	WAYNE GRETZKY, EDM	1982–83
71	JARI KURRI, EDM	1984–85

Brett Hull

Rasslin' with the Russians

When the Soviet Union defeated Canada 7—2 to win the World Hockey Championship in their first foray into the international ice wars in 1954, the vanquished victims were red with embarrassment and white with anger. The following year, a rough 'n' ready band of renegades, dubbed the Penticton V's and led by Bill and Grant Warwick, crossed the ocean to regain Canada's rightful perch atop the world's hockey throne. Combining bone-bruising checking and airtight defense with a fearsome offensive attack, the V's whitewashed the Russians 5—0 in the decisive game to return the crown to Canada.

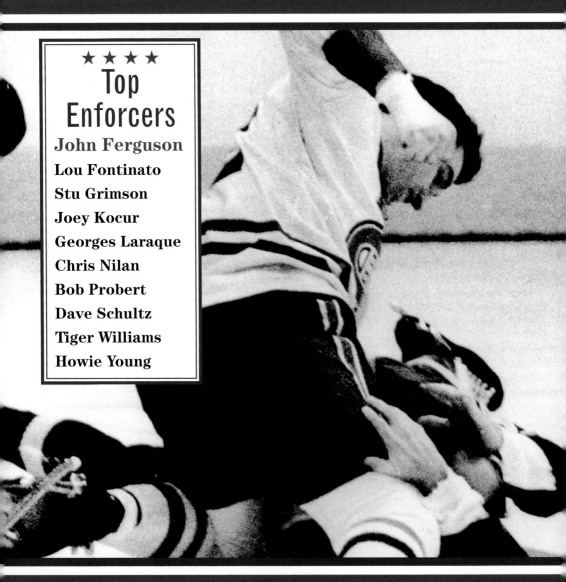

Top Enforcers

John Ferguson

Lou Fontinato

Stu Grimson

Joey Kocur

Georges Laraque

Chris Nilan

Bob Probert

Dave Schultz

Tiger Williams

Howie Young

Cop on the Beat

In the early 1960s, the Montreal Canadiens were looking for an intimidating physical presence to neutralize the new breed of policemen who were stalking the NHL beat. When the Habs heard about John Ferguson, *who was known to terrorize* any teammate that dared fraternize with the opposition, they knew they had found their man. Fergy could shuck knuckles, bruise bones, and light the lamp. During his eight-year reign as the league's top heavyweight harasser, *he never failed* to reach double digits in goals while helping the Canadiens win five Stanley Cup titles.

TALES OF THE
STANLEY CUP

BEDDING THE BOWL

When the New York Islanders finally captured the coveted Cup in 1980, the long-suffering fans were not the only ones who had trouble believing their eyes. Even club catalyst Bryan Trottier wasn't sure where the line between fact and fantasy merged. To erase his doubts, Trots took the Cup home, plunked the bowl in his bed, and slept with his arms around the majestic mug. "I wanted to wake up and find it right beside me" the captain explained. "I didn't want to think I'd just dreamed of this happening."

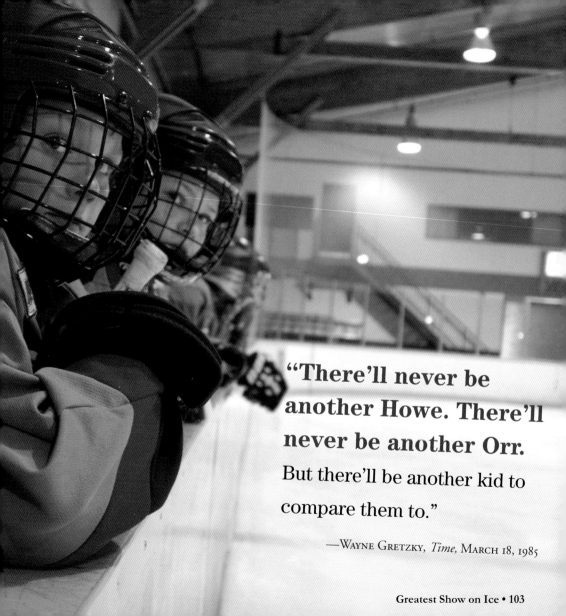

"**There'll never be another Howe. There'll never be another Orr.** But there'll be another kid to compare them to."

—WAYNE GRETZKY, *Time,* MARCH 18, 1985

JUMPIN' AT THE JOE

Opened in 1979 when the Red Wings were not exactly soaring, Joe Louis Arena (named for the legendary heavyweight boxing champion) would be the site of a resurgence in the team's fortunes that would prompt fans to dub Detroit "Hockeytown." The Red Wings had not been Stanley Cup champions since the days of Abel, Lindsay, and Howe in the 1950s, and it took until the end of the 1980s before Steve Yzerman and company began to fill the Joe's 20,000-plus seats on a nightly basis. A 42-year Stanley Cup drought finally ended in 1997, and titles returned to Hockeytown in 1998, 2002, and 2008.

VALERI KHARLAMOV

An on-ice magician, Valeri Kharlamov could weave effortlessly through enemy defenses with speed, skill, and smarts. He played in 436 regular-season games in the Russian Elite League, recording 293 goals in helping the CSKA Red Army team win 11 league championships. Kharlamov participated in 11 consecutive IIHF World and European championships and helped the Soviet Union win the gold medal eight times. He was elected to the Hockey Hall of Fame in 2005.

FACE OF HOCKEY

A young Calgary fan watches the Flames warm up prior to Game 6 of the 2007 Western Conference quarterfinals. The Red Wings proceeded to break his heart, winning in double overtime to eliminate the Flames.

CHAPTER THREE

SLAP SHOTS

"You miss 100 percent of the shots you never take."

—WAYNE GRETKZY

Maurice Richard

"The Rocket"

Known as the "Rocket" for his fiery temper and explosive intensity, Maurice Richard was the dominant right winger in the NHL during the 1940s and 1950s, earning First or Second All-Star Team status 14 times.

Born in Montreal, Richard was destined to and did in fact join the Canadiens, as a 21-year-old in 1942–43. As a sophomore, playing on the Punch Line with Elmer Lach and Toe Blake, the Rocket launched 32 goals. He then scored a dozen playoff goals (including five in a game against Toronto in the semifinals) as the Canadiens took the Stanley Cup.

A thrilling skater who could intimidate the opposition with his deep-set, glaring eyes, Richard attained heroic status in 1944–45 when he scored an unprecedented 50 goals in a single season, beating Boston's Harvey Bennett on the last night of the season to finish the deed. Two years later, he notched 45 goals—again leading the league—and earned his single Hart Trophy.

On November 8, 1952, Richard became the NHL's all-time leading goal-scorer when he netted the 325th tally of his career, passing Nels Stewart. The Rocket remained atop the career goal-scoring chart for the next 11 years until Gordie Howe passed him on November 10, 1963.

Richard was a skilled puck-handler who could skate through the enemy and artfully elude all checkers. He was also a tenacious bulldog who would battle if

> "When Maurice is worked up, his eyes gleam like headlights. . . . Goalies have said he's like a car coming at you at night. He is terrifying."
>
> —Canadiens manager Frank Selke

provoked. In 1954–55, he was banned for the final three games of the season (sparking a riot in Montreal) for fighting with Boston's Hal Laycoe.

On October 19, 1957, Richard scored against goalie Glenn Hall during a 3–1 win over Chicago, sending the Montreal Forum into a frenzy. The tally was his 500th, making him the first NHLer to reach that hallowed mark. Richard retired in 1960 with 544 goals, although he was 35 points shy of the 1,000-point barrier. In 15 trips to the playoffs, Richard put his name on eight Stanley Cups, including five straight beginning in 1955–56.

NHL STATISTICS

REGULAR SEASON						PLAYOFFS				
GP	G	A	PTS	PIM		GP	G	A	PTS	PIM
978	544	421	965	1,285		133	82	44	126	188

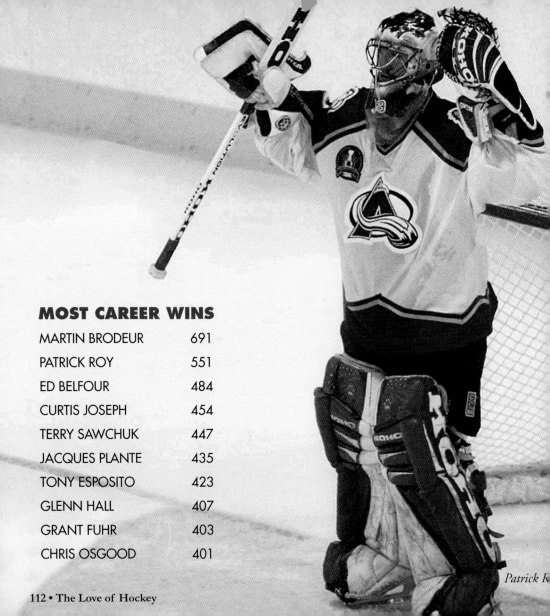

MOST CAREER WINS

MARTIN BRODEUR	691
PATRICK ROY	551
ED BELFOUR	484
CURTIS JOSEPH	454
TERRY SAWCHUK	447
JACQUES PLANTE	435
TONY ESPOSITO	423
GLENN HALL	407
GRANT FUHR	403
CHRIS OSGOOD	401

Patrick R...

Hero Worship

Although he began his career in the Toronto organization, Canadian Dudley "Red" Garrett made his NHL debut with the New York Rangers in the fall of 1942. Like many players before and after him, Garrett abandoned the blades and joined the armed forces. Garrett paid the ultimate price for defending his country when his ship was sunk by a Nazi submarine off the coast of Newfoundland. That dedication is still in evidence today. In 2003, more than two dozen former U.S. college hockey players were members of the U.S. armed forces that helped overthrow the dictatorial regime of Saddam Hussein in Iraq.

Russian Magician

When the 2005—06 NHL season began in earnest, the eyes of every talent adjudicator were focused on Sidney Crosby, the "can't miss kid" of the Pittsburgh Penguins. However, a Russian rocket with the Washington Capitals named Alexander Ovechkin not only stole Crosby's thunder but wrestled the Calder Trophy from the kid as well. Displaying a grin as wide as the Potomac, Ovechkin scored goals with the flair of a magician and the preciseness of a maestro. In a game against Phoenix, with Wayne Gretzky watching from the Coyote bench, Ovechkin scored the highlight-reel goal of the season with an overhand flick of his wrists while sprawled on his back on the ice.

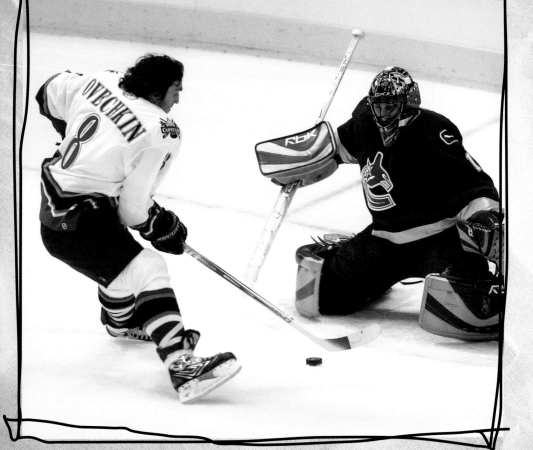

GILBERT PERREAULT

As the graceful and gifted guide of the Buffalo Sabres' famed French Connection trio, Gilbert Perreault played the game with poise, purpose, and passion. Perreault was the NHL's top freshman in 1972–73 and scored at least 30 goals in a season 10 times. He remains the all-time leading scorer in Sabres history with 1,326 points.

What's My Line?

This Motor City trio featured "Terrible" Ted Lindsay (*left*) and Gordie Howe (*middle*) on the wings and revered captain Sid Abel (*right*) at center. In 1949–50, they became the last NHL line to date to finish 1–2–3 in league scoring. What was their line called?

Answer: The Production Line

Mike Modano
"Magic Mo"

On March 17, 2007, this Michigan native scored his 503rd
goal to break Joey Mullen's record for most NHL
tallies by an American-born player.

● ● ●

Holds the Minnesota/Dallas franchise records for games
played (1,241), goals (507), and assists (720).

● ● ●

Led all postseason performers with 18 assists in helping
the Dallas Stars to the Stanley Cup title in 1998–99.

● ● ●

Scored at least 20 goals in 15 of his
21 full seasons in the league.

NHL STATISTICS

REGULAR SEASON					PLAYOFFS				
GP	G	A	PTS	PIM	GP	G	A	PTS	PIM
1,499	561	813	1,374	926	176	58	88	146	128

STANLEY CUP CLASSICS

THE COMEBACK KIDS

In the 1942 Stanley Cup Finals, Detroit coach Jack Adams invented the "dump and chase" method of attack to take advantage of Toronto's slow defense. For the first three games, the Red Wings played their new system to perfection. However, the Leafs made changes for Game 4. They inserted some young guns, benched plodding stars such as Gordie Drillon and Bucko McDonald, and came up with a 4–3 victory. After a 9–3 win in Game 5, it was clear that momentum was changing. By Game 7, a record crowd of 16,218 jammed Maple Leaf Gardens to watch Toronto cap the greatest comeback in hockey history.

CARLTON THE BEAR

The official mascot of the Toronto Maple Leafs, Carlton is named and numbered (No. 60) for the street address where Maple Leaf Gardens was located in downtown Toronto. Well known for a series of comically classic television commercials—in which he travels across Canada harassing other NHL mascots—Carlton hangs out at "The Hangar," the new home of the Leafs at the Air Canada Centre.

GO LEAFS GO! TORONTO MAPLE LEAFS

BRAD PARK

Although he played in the shadow of Bobby Orr during most of his career, Brad Park still managed to be named to an NHL postseason All-Star team seven times. A crafty stickhandler who played with both finesse and feisty determination, Park scored more than 20 goals three times and collected a career-high 82 points for the Rangers in 1973–74.

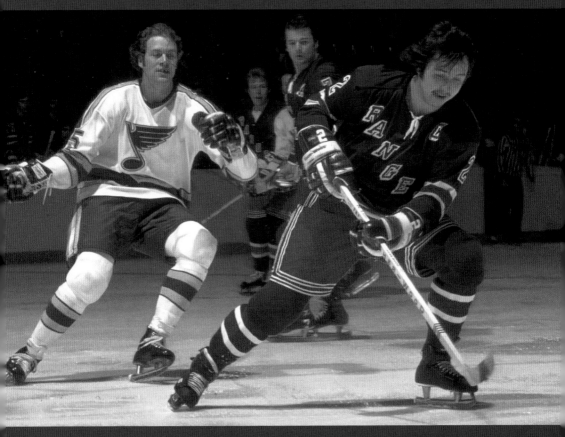

Instant Coffey

Paul Coffey's combination of *instant acceleration,* incomparable agility side-to-side, and the knack for shifting into reverse with ease went a long way toward making him the **NHL's all-time leading scorer** among defensemen. Credited with possessing the "extra gear" common to all classic speed merchants, he also navigated in tight quarters without showing the least discomfort. He was *a one-man skating clinic.*

★ ★ ★ ★
Best Skaters

Pavel Bure
Paul Coffey
Yvan Cournoyer
Sergei Fedorov
Mike Gartner
Bobby Hull
Guy Lafleur
Howie Morenz
Denis Savard
Cyclone Taylor

The Big Train

Lionel Conacher was named Canada's Athlete of the Half-Century (1900–50) for his achievements on a wide variety of playing surfaces. In addition to his Hall of Fame prowess on the ice with a quartet of NHL clubs, Conacher won a Triple-A batting crown in baseball and a Grey Cup crown in football. Nicknamed "The Big Train," Conacher was a tireless competitor. He compiled a perfect 27–0 record as a pro wrestler, packed a punch as the Canadian light-heavyweight boxing champion, and still found the time to excel in professional lacrosse.

FANTASTIC FANS

A native Canadian leaves no doubt who he's rooting for in the gold-medal game of the 2002 Olympics. The Canadian national team defeated the United States 5–2 in Salt Lake City, Utah, to capture the Olympic hockey championship for the first time in 50 years.

Bobby Hull

"The Golden Jet"

Rocket Richard and Boom Boom Geoffrion were the NHL's first two 50-goal scorers, in 1944–45 and 1960–61, respectively. But Bobby Hull, with 15 brilliant seasons in Chicago, was the first NHLer to do it more than once. Known for his speed and great physical strength, Hull scored 50 goals five times, relying on a devastating slap shot to overpower goalies.

An Ontario native, Hull broke into the NHL with the Black Hawks in 1957–58 and was placed on the front line. He emerged as a full-bore superstar in 1959–60, when he scored a league-high 39 goals and won his first Art Ross Trophy with 81 points.

Hull took a back seat to Geoffrion in 1960–61, as the Habs dominated the regular season and Boom Boom stole the show with his 50-goal season. But revenge was sweet for the Hawks, as Chicago eliminated Montreal in the first round of playoffs and then overcame a tough Red Wings squad to annex

> ## "Stopping one of Hull's shots on the pads is like being slugged by a sledge-hammer."
>
> —Opposing goalie Johnny Bower

Ferguson, Hull also played with great sportsmanship, winning a Lady Byng Trophy and his first of two Hart Trophies in 1964–65. He added a

their first Stanley Cup in 23 years. Hull had 14 playoff points and assisted on the Cup-clinching goal in Game 6.

In 1961–62, Hull won his second Art Ross Trophy, scored 50 goals, and led the league with 84 points. Over the next six seasons, Hull paced the NHL in goals five times, including 54 in 1965–66, 52 in 1966–67, and 58 in 1968–69. He added a third Art Ross to his trophy case in 1965–66, with 97 points.

A hard-nosed winger who fought some epic battles with Canadien John

second Hart Trophy the following year.

The Golden Jet scored his 500th NHL goal at the tail end of the 1969–70 season, then added 104 more before dramatically jumping to the World Hockey Association in 1972–73 as that fledgling league's top box-office draw. Hull spent eight years in Winnipeg, scoring 303 goals and 638 points in just 411 games. When the Jets entered the NHL in 1979–80, the 40-year-old Hull returned to his former league. All told, he netted 913 goals in the NHL and WHA.

NHL STATISTICS

REGULAR SEASON						PLAYOFFS				
GP	G	A	PTS	PIM		GP	G	A	PTS	PIM
1,063	610	560	1,170	640		119	62	67	129	102

MAGICAL MOMENTS

HOORAY FOR RAY

No player since Bobby Orr had electrified the Beantown faithful like Ray Bourque, the magnificent Bruin rearguard whose steady consistency, perennial All-Star nominations, and astute hockey sense had helped lead the Bruins to the Stanley Cup Finals in 1988 and 1990. Both times, the Bruins came away without Lord Stanley's Cup, and as Bourque neared the end of his legendary career, even the most diehard Bruins boosters were hoping he would be dispatched to a Stanley Cup contender. In March 2000, Bourque was traded to Colorado. The following season, the Avalanche outlasted the New Jersey Devils in a thrilling seven-game Stanley Cup Finals, giving Bourque the opportunity to retire as a champion.

"What are they gonna want up there next, a bucket of chicken?"

—GLEN SATHER, REFERRING TO THE GOALTENDERS' PRACTICE OF KEEPING WATER BOTTLES ON THE TOP OF THEIR NETS

MARCEL DIONNE

Marcel Dionne was a compact, tenacious fireplug who used his superior strength and low center of gravity to crash and bash his way to the Hockey Hall of Fame. A six-time 50-goal scorer, "Little Beaver" became the last player to win the Art Ross Trophy before a fellow named Gretzky took control of the award. When he retired in 1989, Dionne had scored 731 NHL goals, second only at the time to Gordie Howe's 801.

BULLIES ON BROAD STREET

Though it was the home of the Flyers from 1967 to 1996, the heyday of the Philadelphia Spectrum was the 1970s, when it was the most feared arena in hockey. In front of 17,000 fans hollering for blood, the Flyers delighted their faithful with a combination of talent and toughness that took them to the top. The Broad Street Bullies won Stanley Cups in 1974 and 1975, but perhaps the most memorable moment came on January 11, 1976, when the Flyers became the first NHL team to defeat the Soviet Union's Central Red Army team.

Statue of Kate Smith, who famously sang "God Bless America" prior to important Flyers games in the 1970s

Mais Oui, Manon

Manon Rheaume had already established herself as one of the greatest female goaltenders to ever play the game when the Tampa Bay Lightning signed her as a free agent in August 1992. Rheaume, known in some circles as the "Gorgeous Goaltender," was the first girl to play in the prestigious Quebec City Pee Wee International hockey tournament that had spawned such notables as Wayne Gretzky and Guy Lafleur. Rheaume also garnished attention when she became the first woman to step between the pipes in a QMJHL game. On September 23, 1992, she secured her place in hockey hierarchy by playing in an exhibition game against St. Louis, allowing two goals in 20 minutes of NHL fame.

A 21-year-old Jean Beliveau cuts out news stories about his career to paste into a large scrapbook in December 1952. The young phenom netted 50 goals for the Quebec Aces of the QMHL in 1952–53.

CANDID CAMERA

Don Cherry

Loud and at times obnoxious, "Grapes" Cherry is one of hockey's most vocal and opinionated observers. His *ostentatious clothing* (including loud, checkered jackets; wide, colorful ties; tie pins; and flashy cufflinks) and "old-time hockey" rhetoric combine to give Canadian hockey broadcasts *an almost burlesque aspect.* Once a respected coach who took the Bruins to the brink of the Stanley Cup, "Grapes" is equally famous for his pit bull terrier, Blue.

★ ★ ★ ★
Best Personalities

Don Cherry

Brett Hull

Aurel Joliat

Lanny McDonald

Jacques Plante

Maurice Richard

Jeremy Roenick

Derek Sanderson

Eddie Shore

Gump Worsley

EDDIE SHORE

A surly antagonist who played with a grimace on his face and a bee in his bonnet, Eddie Shore was the NHL's most passionate competitor during the 1930s. This crushing body checker was also known for his daring end-to-end rushes. A four-time league MVP and seven-time All-Star, Shore became an AHL owner and bench boss whose innovative coaching techniques were adapted by coaches around the hockey globe.

HOCKEY HALL OF FAMERS

1) Who is the only member of the Hall of Fame to be born in England?

2) Which three players came out of retirement to play in the NHL after they were inducted into the Hall of Fame?

3) Who is the only Hall of Fame member to win the Lady Byng Trophy as a defenseman and a forward?

4) Which two Hall of Famers were named to the NHL All-Star Team as both a forward and a defenseman?

5) Which member of the Hall of Fame is the only defenseman in NHL history to play an entire season without serving a single minute in the penalty box?

6) Who is the only Hall of Famer to have his name engraved on the Stanley Cup as a player, coach, and general manager?

Answers: 1) "Mean" Joe Hall; 2) Gordie Howe, Guy Lafleur, and Mario Lemieux; 3) Red Kelly; 4) Neil Colville and Dit Clapper; 5) Bill Quackenbush; 6) Jack Adams

Phil Esposito
"The Slot Machine"

Only four men in NHL history scored more goals than Phil Esposito. The leader of the Big, Bad Bruins of the 1970s, Esposito had a simple plan: Fire the puck quickly on net, and the rest would take care of itself.

Though his game was neither complex nor a thing of beauty, Espo was arguably the most dangerous weapon of his day. In 1970–71, he shattered the single-season goal mark when he scored 76 times.

Camping in front of the enemy net, Espo used his long reach and powerful wrists to whip home passes from his two board-crashing worker bees, Wayne Cashman and Ken Hodge. And heaven help the goalie who left a loose puck in the slot. Espo's specialty was shoveling in rebounds, regardless of the abuse heaped on him by defensemen.

In 1964–65, his first full season in the NHL, Esposito centered a line with Bobby Hull and amassed 32 assists. After four modest seasons, he was traded to Boston. In Beantown, Espo blossomed, recording career highs in goals (35) and points (84) while leading the NHL in assists (49). In 1968–69, he won his first scoring title (126 points) and the first of two Hart Trophies. Never had a change of scenery netted better results.

With Bobby Orr on defense, Gerry Cheevers in goal, and Espo on the front line, the Big, Bad Bruins dominated. In 1969–70, Esposito's production fell to 99 points, but he did lead the NHL in goals (43). In the 1970 playoffs, he ripped 13 goals and 27 points in 14 games to lead in all categories. Riding Espo's broad shoulders, Boston won its first Stanley Cup in 29 years.

"Jesus Saves, Espo Scores on the Rebound"

—Popular bumper sticker in Boston

Over the next four years, Esposito won four Art Ross Trophies as the NHL's top point-getter. In 1970–71, he tallied an NHL-record 152 points. A year later, he scored 66 goals, led the NHL with 133 points, and powered Boston to its second Cup in three years.

Espo won two more scoring titles (1972–73 and 1973–74) and a second Hart Trophy (1973–74) before his shocking trade to the Rangers for Brad Park and Jean Ratelle in 1975. Though he never found the 100-point range again, he enjoyed one last 40-goal season (42 tallies) in 1978–79.

NHL STATISTICS

REGULAR SEASON					PLAYOFFS				
GP	G	A	PTS	PIM	GP	G	A	PTS	PIM
1,282	717	873	1,590	910	130	61	76	137	138

FACE OF HOCKEY

Anaheim's Teemu Selanne sports a black eye in Game 3 of the 2007 Western Conference semifinals against Vancouver. Selanne saw well enough in Game 4 to score a key goal in a 3–2 Ducks victory.

LARRY ROBINSON

Known as "Big Bird" during his Hall of Fame career with Montreal and Los Angeles because of his wide wingspan, Larry Robinson (*#19*) twirled his way to six Stanley Cup titles as a player and added another championship as the head coach of the New Jersey Devils. The two-time Norris Trophy winner fashioned a remarkable plus/minus mark of +120 during the 1976–77 campaign.

MAGICAL MOMENTS

6–5, 6–5, 6–5

Every game of the finals of the 1987 Canada Cup tournament between Canada and the Soviet Union was frantically paced, action-packed, and decided by a 6–5 score. The Russians used an overtime marker by Alexander Semak to eke out a 6–5 victory in the series lid-lifter, and Canada countered with a double-overtime goal by Mario Lemieux to square the set at one. The decisive match, which featured furious end-to-end action and a flurry of lead changes, was knotted at 5–5 before Lemieux parlayed a classic cross-ice feed from Wayne Gretzky into the top shelf of the Soviet net. The goal gave Canada a 6–5 victory and their second consecutive Canada Cup triumph.

Wayne Gretzky and Mario Lemieux (center)
celebrating a goal against the Soviet Union

STANLEY CUP CLASSICS

BULLIES AND BRUISERS

In 1973–74, in just their seventh season, the Philadelphia Flyers became the first NHL expansion team to win the Stanley Cup with a six-game victory over Boston in one of the toughest Finals in history. Though the Flyers were known more for their muscle than their majesty, it was the team's two most talented players who made the difference. Center Bobby Clarke supplied the offense (including a key overtime winner in Game 2) and goalie Bernie Parent made sure Clarke's points counted. Parent's shutout in Game 6 sealed a 1–0 victory and capped a Conn Smythe performance.

★ ★ ★ ★
1974 Stanley Cup Finals

May 7	Philadelphia 2 at Boston 3
May 9	Philadelphia 3 at Boston 2 OT
May 12	Boston 1 at Philadelphia 4
May 14	Boston 2 at Philadelphia 4
May 16	Philadelphia 1 at Boston 5
May 19	Boston 0 at Philadelphia 1

TALES OF THE
STANLEY CUP

KICKING THE CUP

For some reason, the Ottawa Silver Seven in 1905 felt it necessary to use the Cup as a football following a lively night of celebratory swilling and spilling. After remarking that the shape of the bowl was not unlike that of a rugby ball, one of the soused Seven tried to punt the prize over the Rideau Canal in Ottawa. Although his aim was true, his skills were shoddy and the Cup landed on the frozen expanse of the canal. Unable to locate the chalice in the darkness, the maligned mug remained in its icy tomb until the next day, when sober heads prevailed and the mug was recovered.

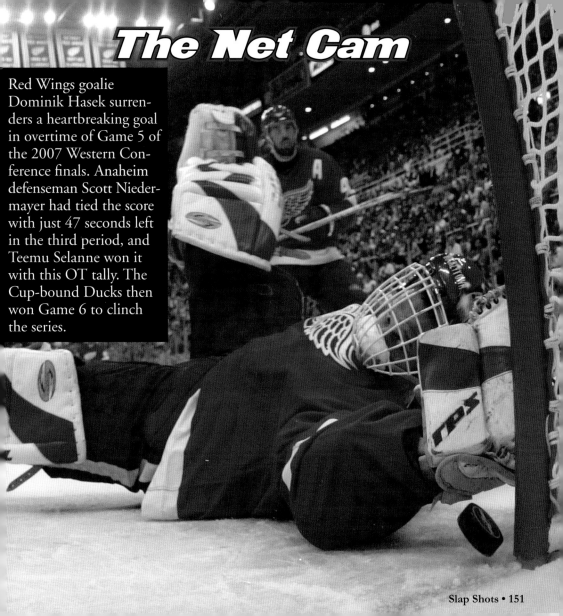

The Net Cam

Red Wings goalie Dominik Hasek surrenders a heartbreaking goal in overtime of Game 5 of the 2007 Western Conference finals. Anaheim defenseman Scott Niedermayer had tied the score with just 47 seconds left in the third period, and Teemu Selanne won it with this OT tally. The Cup-bound Ducks then won Game 6 to clinch the series.

Ted Lindsay

"Terrible Ted"

Nicknamed Terrible Ted because of his feisty, aggressive on-ice nature, Lindsay was selected to the NHL First All-Star Team eight times.

● ● ●

A member of Detroit's famed Production Line with Gordie Howe and Sid Abel, Lindsay was named to the *Sports Illustrated* All-Time Dream Team in 1994.

● ● ●

Recorded at least 20 goals in 11 different seasons. Led the league in points (78) in 1949–50 and assists (55) in 1956–57.

● ● ●

After winning four Stanley Cups with Detroit, Lindsay was the third player to be inducted into the Hockey Hall of Fame without having to serve the mandatory three-year waiting period.

NHL STATISTICS

REGULAR SEASON					PLAYOFFS				
GP	G	A	PTS	PIM	GP	G	A	PTS	PIM
1,068	379	472	851	1,808	133	47	49	96	194

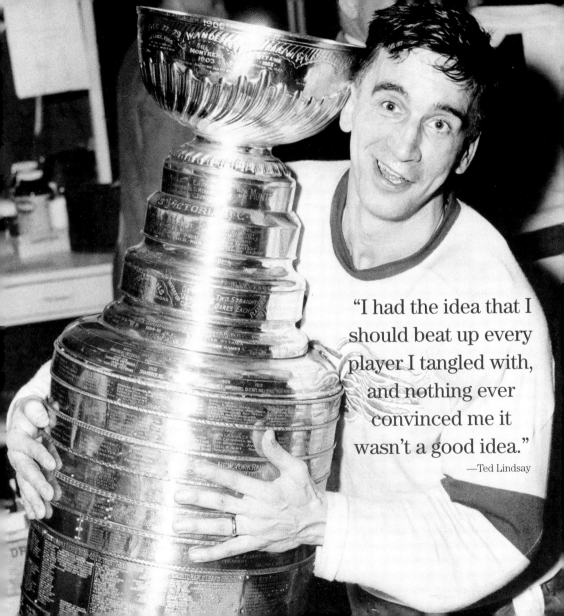

"I had the idea that I should beat up every player I tangled with, and nothing ever convinced me it wasn't a good idea."

—Ted Lindsay

Who Is That Masked Man?

Jacques Plante changed the face of hockey on November 1, 1959, when he donned a crude mask and ended the era of the bare-faced crease cop. In a game against the New York Rangers, a wicked backhand shot off the stick of Andy Bathgate ripped a swath of flesh off Plante's face. Plante returned to the crease wearing a mask and went on to win the match. Despite the protests of his coach, Plante continued to wear the facial protection. When he helped the Habs sweep the Maple Leafs in the 1960 Stanley Cup Finals, he served notice that the mask did not deter a goalie's effectiveness and ushered in the modern era of NHL goaltending.

"When I first put on the mask, the boys all told me I would scare the women. They wouldn't come to see the games anymore. I'll tell you something, if I went on the way I was going, pretty soon my face would look worse than the mask."

—JACQUES PLANTE ON
WEARING HIS MASK

Two for Toews

Since the rules on participating in the World Hockey Championships were relaxed in the 1970s to allow professional players to compete, the squad that has represented Canada at the tournament has been packed with NHL stars. Rarely has a roster spot been available to a player without NHL experience. Jonathan Toews changed that dynamic in 2007. After leading Canada in scoring at the World Junior Championships in January, Toews was asked to join the senior squad at the World Championships in May. The second youngest player to ever wear Canada's colors at the event, Toews became the first player to win a gold medal at both tournaments in the same year.

Toews scoring against Sweden in the 2007 World Championships

Last but Not Least

When Dave Taylor was selected 210th overall by the L.A. Kings in the 1975 draft, few prognosticators believed he would ever play a shift in the NHL. Taylor, who had set a litany of school scoring records during his three full semesters at Clarkson University, turned the skeptics into believers by scoring at least 20 goals in 12 different NHL seasons while twice climbing the 100-point ladder. He wound up playing 1,111 NHL games, all with Los Angeles. Taylor, whose No. 18 was retired by the Kings in 1995, is the only player in NHL history to be drafted 200th or lower and collect 1,000 career points.

MOST WINS IN A SEASON

MARTIN BRODEUR, NJ	2006–07
BRADEN HOLTBY, WASH	2015–16
ROBERTO LUONGO, VAN	2006–07
BERNIE PARENT, PHI	1973–74
EVGENI NABOKOV, PIT	2007–08
MARTIN BRODEUR, NJ	2009–10
MIKKA KIPRUSOFF, CAL	2008–09
MARTIN BRODEUR, NJ	2007-08
EVGENI NABOKOV, PIT	2009–10
CAREY PRICE, MTL	2014–15

Martin Brodeur

CHAPTER FOUR

POWER PLAYS

"There are two types of forwards.
Scorers and bangers. Scorers
score and bangers bang."

—KEN DRYDEN

Jari Kurri

"The Fantastic Finn"

The first European-trained player to score 500 goals, Kurri
retired as the highest-scoring European player in NHL
history with 1,398 points.

● ● ●

Won four Stanley Cup titles as a member of the
Edmonton Oilers.

● ● ●

Named to the NHL First All-Star Team in 1984–85 and
1986–87. Selected to the Second All-Star Team three times.

● ● ●

Scored at least 50 goals in four consecutive seasons,
including a career-high 71 goals in 1984–85. Reached the
20-goal plateau 13 times.

NHL STATISTICS

REGULAR SEASON					PLAYOFFS				
GP	G	A	PTS	PIM	GP	G	A	PTS	PIM
1,251	601	797	1,398	545	200	106	127	233	123

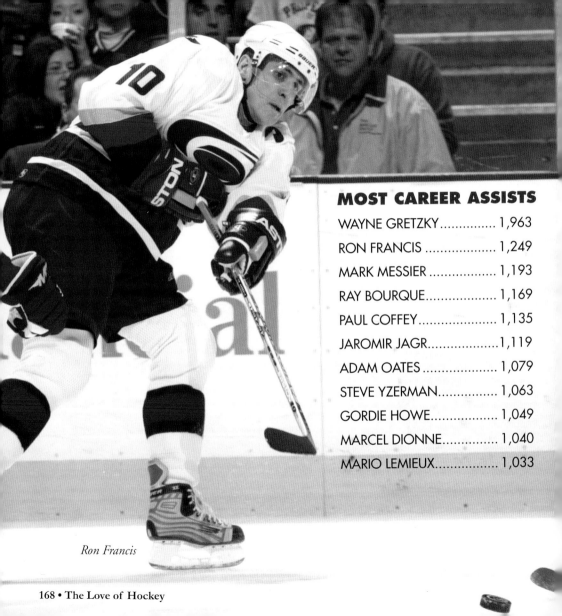

MOST CAREER ASSISTS

WAYNE GRETZKY	1,963
RON FRANCIS	1,249
MARK MESSIER	1,193
RAY BOURQUE	1,169
PAUL COFFEY	1,135
JAROMIR JAGR	1,119
ADAM OATES	1,079
STEVE YZERMAN	1,063
GORDIE HOWE	1,049
MARCEL DIONNE	1,040
MARIO LEMIEUX	1,033

Ron Francis

The One-Puck Game

In the early days of hockey, spectators were expected to return any puck that left the ice and went into the crowd. As one can imagine, some hometown enthusiasts were reluctant to return the disk to the referee if their beloved squad was on the negative side of the score sheet. That rule of return was no longer in practice when the Los Angeles Kings and Minnesota North Stars did battle on November 10, 1979, but it wouldn't have mattered anyway. On that evening, the puck stayed in play for the entire game. It is the only game in modern-day history in which the same puck was slapped around for a full 60 minutes.

Gordie Howe

"Mr. Hockey"

So many moments contributed to the enduring legend of "Mr. Hockey." There was the night he pummeled enforcer Lou Fontinato into a bloody pulp...the game he surpassed Rocket Richard as the NHL's all-time leading goal-scorer... the day he debuted with his sons, Mark and Marty...and the night he made his triumphant return to the NHL at the unheard-of age of 51.

A Saskatchewan native, Howe debuted in the NHL in 1946–47 with the Red Wings. In his first three NHL seasons, he scored seven, 16, and 12 goals and rarely looked like a world-beater. Then, in 1949–50, Howe ripped 35 goals and finished third overall in points (68) behind Production Line mates Ted Lindsay (78) and Sid Abel (69).

In 1949–50, the Red Wings finished atop the league standings and were favorites to win the Stanley Cup. But they had to do it without Howe. In Game 1 of the semifinals, he threw a check at Toronto's Teeder Kennedy, missed, and flew into the boards, fracturing his skull. Emergency surgery saved his life, but he missed Detroit's first Stanley Cup in seven years.

Over the next five years, Detroit won three more Stanley Cups (1952, '54, and '55) and Howe established his credentials as a bona fide superstar. In 1950–51, he won his first of six Art Ross Trophies, leading the NHL in goals (43), assists (43), and points (86). The following season (1951–52), he won his second

> ### "They should have two pucks when he's out there. One for him and one for the rest of the players."
> —Toronto Maple Leafs coach Hap Day, 1950

Ross Trophy (with 86 points) and took home his first Hart Trophy as league MVP.

Howe continued to shine well into the 1960s. On November 10, 1963, he scored his 545th goal to pass Rocket Richard's NHL record. He was named league MVP in 1952, 1953, 1957, 1958, 1960, and 1963.

Howe retired in 1971, but three years later, he returned to play with his sons in the WHA. And after six years in Houston and New England, he reentered the NHL in 1979–80. He was long hailed as the greatest player in history, a claim he would hold until the emergence of Wayne Gretzky.

NHL STATISTICS

REGULAR SEASON					PLAYOFFS				
GP	G	A	PTS	PIM	GP	G	A	PTS	PIM
1,767	801	1,049	1,850	1,685	157	68	92	160	220

STANLEY CUP CLASSICS

DOUSING THE FLAMES

The Calgary Flames had missed the playoffs for seven straight years. But in 2004, as the postseason victories piled up, Flames fans were painting Calgary red. No Canadian team had even reached the Finals since 1994, and fans all across the country got caught up in the frenzy. The Flames took a 3–2 lead through the first five Stanley Cup contests against Tampa Bay. They had a chance to win it at home in Game 6 until NHL scoring leader Martin St. Louis extinguished the fire with a double-overtime winner for Tampa Bay. The Lightning won Game 7 for their first Stanley Cup title.

★ ★ ★ ★
2004 Stanley Cup Finals

Calgary 4 at Tampa Bay 1
Calgary 1 at Tampa Bay 4
Tampa Bay 0 at Calgary 3
Tampa Bay 1 at Calgary 0
Calgary 3 at Tampa Bay 2 OT
Tampa Bay 3 at Calgary 2 2OT
Calgary 1 at Tampa Bay 2

Martin St. Louis attempting to score in Game 7 of the Finals

Last at Bat

A graduate of Denver University, Bill "Bat" Masterton was signed by the Montreal Canadiens, but the Habs' depth of talent kept him off the NHL payroll. Instead of languishing in the minors, he chose to join the U.S. national team and play in the amateur ranks. When the Minnesota North Stars were awarded an expansion franchise, Masterton was given the chance to play in the NHL, and in 1967 he scored the first goal in franchise history. During a game against Oakland on January 13, 1968, he fell heavily to the ice and suffered a head injury. He died two days later. The Bill Masterton Memorial Trophy is named in his honor.

HARVEY THE HOUND

Named the top mascot in the NHL in 2004, Harvey is well known for his billowing tongue and sarcastic mannerisms. The Calgary mascot's persistent yammering pushed Edmonton's head coach over the edge in January 2003. Craig MacTavish got so mad that he ripped the tongue right out of the poor pooch's mouth.

LES GLORIEUX

The Montreal Canadiens of the 1970s were fueled by a lanky goaltender with the vocabulary of a lawyer (Ken Dryden), a trio of defensemen who zealously protected their own zone, and a flashy offense that mixed speed, dexterity, and determination. In the waning moments of their seven-game tussle with Boston in the 1979 semifinals, it appeared their three-year grip on the Stanley Cup would finally be loosened, as the Bruins led by a goal. However, Boston was whistled for having too many men on the ice. With the extra skater, Guy Lafleur took a pass, stepped over the blueline, and rifled a shot just inside the goalpost. Montreal won in overtime and then marched past the Rangers to win their fourth straight championship.

What's My Line?

In 1939–40, Boston Bruins linemates Milt Schmidt (*left*), Woody Dumart (*center*), and Bobby Bauer (*right*) finished 1–2–3 in the NHL in scoring. What was the name of this all-German line?

Answer: The Kraus Line

Nicklas Lidstrom

"Super Swede"

The first European-trained player to win the Conn Smythe
Trophy as playoff MVP (2002), Lidstrom was named to NHL
First All-Star Team ten times.

● ● ●

Won the Norris Trophy seven times in the 21st century and
holds the Red Wings record for points in a season by
a defenseman (80).

● ● ●

Named captain of the Red Wings following the retirement of
Steve Yzerman.

● ● ●

After winning three Cups with Detroit, Nicklas copped an
Olympic gold medal with Sweden in 2006.

NHL STATISTICS

REGULAR SEASON					PLAYOFFS				
GP	G	A	PTS	PIM	GP	G	A	PTS	PIM
1,564	264	878	1,142	514	263	54	129	183	76

A cerebral maestro who combines skill, speed, and smarts with a disciplined and sharp focus, Lidstrom became only the fourth defenseman to win the Norris Trophy in three straight years when he took home the hardware in 2002–03.

HALL OF FAME TREASURES

THREE GOALS IN 21 SECONDS
AN NHL RECORD FOR MOSIENKO

1914 STANLEY CUP FINAL

Above: *On March 23, 1952, Chicago's Bill Mosienko set an NHL record by scoring three goals within 21 seconds against the Rangers.* Far left: *On February 14, 1934, the NHL staged its first All-Star Game as a benefit for Maple Leafs star Ace Bailey, who had been forced into retirement (and nearly killed) by a vicious check by Boston's Eddie Shore.* Immediate left: *The city of Toronto celebrated its first Stanley Cup in 1914, when the Blueshirts of the NHA defeated Victoria of the PCHA three games to none.*

CHARLIE CONACHER

One of the NHL's first power forwards, Charlie Conacher used his superior size and strength to muscle his way to the top of the NHL's goal-scoring ladder five times during his NHL career. Nicknamed "Big Bomber," Conacher utilized a devastating wrist shot to win a pair of scoring tiles and earn five berths on the postseason NHL All-Star Teams.

MAGICAL MOMENTS

ROLLING DOUBLES

Scoring in overtime can vault a role player from the files of the
unknown to the height of glory. That spotlight glows even brighter
in the Stanley Cup Finals, in which only two players have managed
to score two overtime goals in the same year. In 1950, Don "Bones"
Raleigh connected for a pair of extra-time markers for the New York
Rangers that allowed the Broadway Blues to stretch their series against
Detroit to the limit. In 1993, Montreal's John LeClair pocketed a pair of
overtime winners as the Habs crowned the L.A. Kings in five games to
win the 23rd championship in team history.

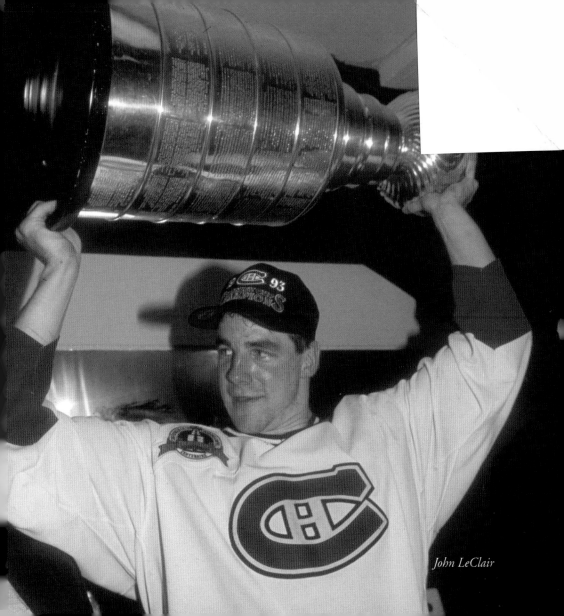

John LeClair

STANLEY CUP CLASSICS

BROADWAY BEDLAM

After finally bringing the championship to Broadway in 1994, Mark Messier and Brian Leetch made sure the vaunted majestic mug received the media attention it deserved. They escorted Stanley to the *Late Show with David Letterman*, where it was featured in a segment called Stupid Cup Tricks. Ed Olczyk carted the Cup to the Belmont racetrack and allowed the 1994 Kentucky Derby winner, Go for Gin, to use it as a festive feedbag. Teammates Brian Noonan and Nick Kypreos stuffed the silverware with raw clams and oysters for the horse's fishy feast.

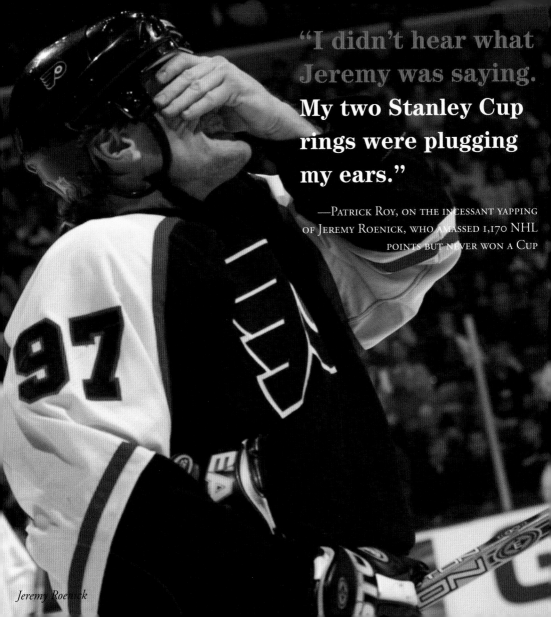

"I didn't hear what Jeremy was saying. **My two Stanley Cup rings were plugging my ears.**"

—PATRICK ROY, ON THE INCESSANT YAPPING OF JEREMY ROENICK, WHO AMASSED 1,170 NHL POINTS BUT NEVER WON A CUP

Jeremy Roenick

True Grit

There's no pleasure in pain, but watching Cam Neely thrive and survive in the NHL despite a litany of breaks and aches brought smiles to fans' faces in the 1980s and '90s. The longtime Boston Bruin played with *reckless abandon,* barging through enemy defenses and slamming opposing forwards. "Bam-Bam" Cam earned a reputation as *the grittiest player in the NHL.*

★ ★ ★ ★
Grittiest Players

Bobby Clarke
Bill Ezinicki
Gordie Howe
Ted Lindsay
Mark Messier
Cam Neely
Terry O'Reilly
Marcel Pronovost
Maurice Richard
Gary Roberts

Cam Neely

Bronco Busting

A referee's mistake helped rob Boston's Bronco Horvath of the NHL scoring title in 1959—60. During a game against Chicago, Horvath was sprinting in on a clear breakaway when Black Hawk defenseman Al Arbour hurled his cue across the ice and pocketed the puck off Horvath's stick. The referee in charge, Dalton McArthur, correctly awarded a penalty shot, but instead of giving the free throw to Horvath, he allowed the Chicago coach to choose the shooter. The Black Hawk bench boss appointed a seldom-used journeyman named Larry Leach, whose feeble attempt was easily smothered by goalie Glenn Hall. Horvath missed winning that season's scoring title by a single point.

ALEX DELVECCHIO

An stellar two-way performer who exuded class, Alex "Fats" Delvecchio spent 24 seasons with the Detroit Red Wings, an NHL record for longevity with one franchise. Known for his playmaking, cool demeanor, and astute advice in the dressing room, Delvecchio trailed only Gordie Howe in NHL annals in games (1,549), assists (825), and points (1,281) when he retired in 1973. Delvecchio, who collected a career-high 71 points at age 42, played in 13 All-Star Games and scored at least 20 goals 13 times.

The Grand Slam of Hockey

It is unclear whether Wendell Young displayed any prowess on the baseball diamond, but he is the only player to hit hockey's version of the grand slam by winning a championship ring in four different leagues. He skated away with the Memorial Cup, the symbol of junior hockey supremacy, as a member of the OHL's Kitchener Rangers. Young later captured the Calder Cup with the AHL's Hershey Bears, sipped champagne from the Stanley Cup as a Penguin in Pittsburgh, and toasted the Turner Cup with the IHL's Chicago Wolves.

Wendell Young

SPECTACULAR SCORING

1) Who holds the record for the fastest three goals in NHL history?

2) Which WHA player (and former Maple Leaf) matched Darryl Sittler's NHL record of 10 points in a single game?

3) Who holds the NHL record for most goals in a road game?

4) Which player has been a member of the only two NHL teams to overcome a five-goal deficit in the third period and win the game?

5) Which team has scored the most goals in a single NHL game?

6) Who is the only player to score a hat trick in overtime?

Answers: 1) Bill Mosienko, 21 seconds; 2) Jim Harrison, Edmonton Oilers; 3) Red Berenson, six; 4) Al MacInnis, with Calgary and St. Louis; 5) Montreal Canadiens, 16 ; 6) Ken Doraty, who scored thrice for Toronto on January 16, 1934, during a 10-minute overtime period

FACE OF HOCKEY

A Czech hockey fan sheds tears while watching the final match of the 2006 World Championships between the Czech Republic and Sweden. The Swedes prevailed 4–0.

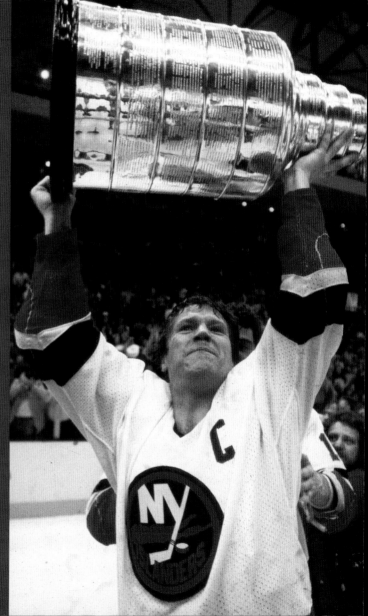

"Often I'm asked which Cup I fancy the most and I often reply by saying, 'It's like having four children. Which one do you love the most?' All are totally different, but the first one is always very special because it is the first one."

—Denis Potvin

Denis Potvin

"The Anchor"

The first overall selection in the 1973 amateur draft, Potvin
won the Calder Trophy in 1973–74 and the Norris Trophy in
1975–76, 1977–78, and 1978–79.

● ● ●

Was a member of four Stanley Cup-winning teams with the
New York Islanders.

● ● ●

Became the first NHL rearguard to reach 1,000 points.
Retired as the NHL's all-time leader in goals (310), assists
(742), and points (1,050) by a defenseman.

● ● ●

Scored at least 20 goals nine times and was named to the
NHL First All-Star Team five times.

NHL STATISTICS

REGULAR SEASON					PLAYOFFS				
GP	G	A	PTS	PIM	GP	G	A	PTS	PIM
1,060	310	742	1,052	1,356	185	56	108	164	253

JOE MALONE

Malone was known as "The Phantom" for his ability to disappear in heavy traffic only to materialize in front of the enemy cage with the puck on his stick and a glint in his eye. He was the NHL's first scoring leader, netting 44 goals in 20 games (including three five-goal games) for the Montreal Canadiens in 1917–18. His 2.20 goals-per-game ratio that season has never been matched.

FANTASTIC FANS

Senators fans Bryanna, Brian, and Steve Lester root their hearts out for the Ottawa Senators prior to the team's first playoff game, against Tampa Bay, in 2006. Ottawa won the series but was eliminated by Buffalo in the next round.

DA GARDEN

A blue-collar facility for working-class fans, the Boston Garden wasn't glamorous, but it was beloved by the Bruins faithful. The Garden was built for boxing, and the ice surface was smaller than most other NHL arenas. Fans in the stands were practically on top of the players, with the "Gallery Gods" hollering their support from on high. Originally opened in 1928, the Garden retained its feeling of Eddie Shore and old-time hockey through the lean years of the 1950s and '60s. Bobby Orr and Phil Esposito brought championship glory to the arena in the 1970s.

MAGICAL MOMENTS

BOBBY ON THE BLUELINE

The game had never seen anyone like him, before or since. When Bobby Orr reconstructed the role of rearguards by combining offensive flair, picture-perfect passing, and gritty hard-nosed work along the blueline, he changed the face and the pace of the game. In 1969–70, Orr accomplished a feat that even the most ardent of enthusiasts never would have thought possible: He won the scoring title with a league-leading 87 assists and 120 points. The following season, he set up his teammates a record 102 times. In 1974–75, Orr captured his second Art Ross Trophy with 135 points, a seemingly unbreakable record for a defenseman.

"No matter how the team plays in front of me, I have the last say on the puck. If it gets past me, it's my fault."

—Hall of Fame goalie Tony Esposito

Tony Esposito

Mario Lemieux

"The Magnificent"

He was majestic in flight, pulling fans out of their seats with his powerful skating strides, magnificent speed, and delicately deft dekes and feints. He was Mario Lemieux, the first "Next One" and the only one who not only lived up to the hype but actually surpassed it.

During his freshman NHL campaign with the Pittsburgh Penguins in 1984–85, Lemieux became just the third rookie in league history to record 100 points. He would reach the century mark in points 10 times during his career, earn a pair of Stanley Cup rings, win an Olympic gold medal, capture six scoring titles, and set a plethora of NHL records. Midway through a monumental 199-point season in 1988–89, Lemieux scored five goals in a game in five different ways—even strength, power play, short-handed, penalty shot, and empty net.

When the Penguins were finally ready to ascend to Stanley Cup heights, it was Super Mario who carried them there. In the 1991 playoffs, Lemieux notched 44 points in 23 games as Pittsburgh won its first Stanley Cup. The following season, Lemieux repeated his postseason heroics, pocketing a second consecutive playoff MVP award as the Penguins won their final 11 postseason games to claim the Stanley Cup.

After securing another scoring title with 160 points in 1992–93, Lemieux was sidelined by recurring back trouble. Shortly after returning to active duty, he was diagnosed with Hodgkin's disease, and the resulting treatment forced him to miss the majority of the 1993–94 season and the entire 1994–95 schedule. Incredibly, Lemieux returned to top form

and won another pair of scoring crowns before his health problems overcame his desire. He reluctantly decided to retire, becoming the first NHL player to leave the game after winning the league scoring title.

Though he left the ice, Lemieux was active behind the scenes, orchestrating a deal to purchase the Penguins to keep the club in Pittsburgh. But the boardroom boredom reignited his competitive juices, and he became just the third player to return to active duty after being inducted into the Hockey Hall of Fame. His legendary skills may have eroded, but his passion remained resolutely intact. Lemieux continued to light up NHL arenas until he packed away the blades for good midway through the 2005–06 season.

NHL STATISTICS

REGULAR SEASON					PLAYOFFS				
GP	G	A	PTS	PIM	GP	G	A	PTS	PIM
915	690	1,033	1,723	834	107	76	96	172	87

MOST ASSISTS IN A SEASON

163	WAYNE GRETZKY, EDM	1985–86
135	WAYNE GRETZKY, EDM	1984–85
125	WAYNE GRETZKY, EDM	1982–83
122	WAYNE GRETZKY, LA	1990–91
121	WAYNE GRETZKY, EDM	1986–87
120	WAYNE GRETZKY, EDM	1981–82
118	WAYNE GRETZKY, EDM	1983–84
114	WAYNE GRETZKY, LA	1988–89
114	MARIO LEMIEUX, PIT	1988–89
109	WAYNE GRETZKY, EDM	1980–81
109	WAYNE GRETZKY, EDM	1987–88

Wayne Gretzky

"The highest compliment that you can pay me is to say that I work hard every day, that I never dog it."

—Wayne Gretzky

Chicago Blackhawks

Team of the '10s

A hard salary cap has introduced a new level of parity in the NHL, giving teams the ability to climb from the bottom to the top — or vice versa — far more easily than they could in the days of the mighty Canadiens, Islanders, or Oilers dynasties of the 20th century.

It makes what the Chicago Blackhawks have done in recent years that much more impressive. With Stanley Cup championships in 2010, '13, and '15, the Hawks have to be considered the greatest NHL dynasty since the Gretzky-Messier days in Edmonton in the late 1980s.

Under Coach Joel Quenneville,

the Hawks of Jonathan Toews, Patrick Kane and Duncan Keith have owned the postseason with a unique blend of offensive firepower and two-way grit — not to mention the most raucous National Anthem fan behavior south of the border.

WINDY CITY WINNING:

- 2009: Western Finals
- 2010: Stanley Cup Champions
- 2011: Western Quarterfinals
- 2012: Western Quarterfinals
- 2013: Stanley Cup Champions
- 2014: Western Finals
- 2015: Stanley Cup Champions

SCOTT STEVENS

Known for his bruising, bone-crunching body checks and his poise along the blueline, Scott Stevens captained the New Jersey Devils to three Stanley Cup championships. After starting his career as a flashy, offensive defender who reached double digits in goals in nine of his first 12 NHL seasons, Stevens reinvented himself as a solid, steady, stay-at-home blueliner who crushed any opponent who dared to skate into his kitchen.

The Net Cam

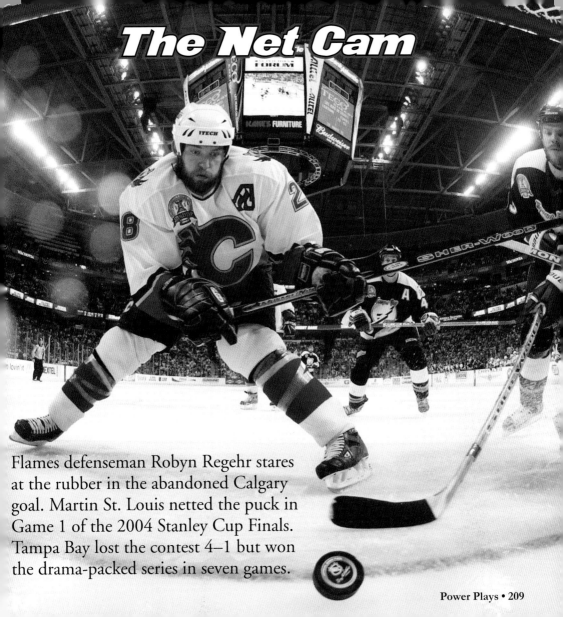

Flames defenseman Robyn Regehr stares at the rubber in the abandoned Calgary goal. Martin St. Louis netted the puck in Game 1 of the 2004 Stanley Cup Finals. Tampa Bay lost the contest 4–1 but won the drama-packed series in seven games.

CHAPTER FIVE

LAST LINE OF DEFENSE

"How would you like a job where, every time you make a mistake, a big red light goes on and 18,000 people boo?"

—JACQUES PLANTE

Patrick Roy

"St. Patrick"

Patrick Roy was the first of the new wave of netminders to employ the butterfly style. Although other practitioners had used a similar method, Roy was the first goaltender who consistently spread his pads from post to post to cut off the bottom corners of the net. He covered the rest of the cage with his bulky upper torso and razor-sharp reflexes. With this unique style, a feisty exterior, and a calm demeanor, Roy became the winningest goalie in NHL history.

Roy took over the goaltending duties of the Montreal Canadiens in 1985–86 and quickly established himself as the club's No. 1 pivot between the pipes. During the 1986 playoffs, he backstopped the Canadiens to an unlikely Stanley Cup victory, earning the Conn Smythe Trophy as a just reward. That postseason performance and his unorthodox goaltending made him a crowd favorite in the Montreal Forum and motivated hundreds of would-be netminders to copy his butterfly-first style.

Roy led the league in goals-against average in 1988–89, a season in which he guided the Canadiens to the Stanley Cup Finals. In 1992–93, Roy elevated his postseason heroics to a mythical level by going 10–0 in overtime en route to the team's 23rd championship. Dubbed "St. Patrick," Roy raised expectations for himself and his teammates that would prove impossible to maintain.

Early in the 1995–96 season, those pressures reached a boiling point, and Roy demanded to be traded to escape the frenzy that surrounded him. Days later, he was dispatched to the Colorado Avalanche, who had just relocated to the mile-high state from Quebec City. The Avalanche, who were already loaded with exceptional talent, climbed on the St. Patrick bandwagon and rode it to the first Stanley Cup title in franchise history.

Roy remained in Colorado for the rest of his career, winning another Stanley Cup in 2001. In addition to his four championships and a trio of Conn Smythe awards, Roy became the first goaltender to play in 1,000 NHL games and recorded a league-record 551 wins.

> "There are certain athletes, like Patrick, who are purebreds. They're intense. They're winners."
>
> —Former Canadiens coach Jacques Demers

NHL STATISTICS

REGULAR SEASON					PLAYOFFS				
W	L	T	SO	GAA	W	L	T	SO	GAA
1,029	551	315	66	2.54	151	94	0	23	2.30

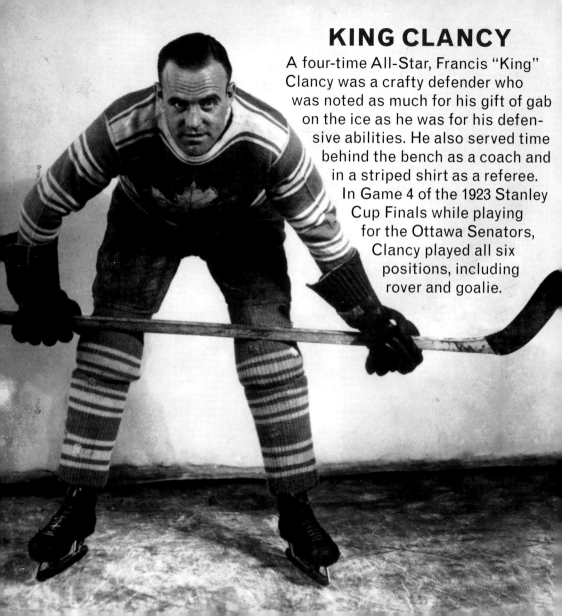

KING CLANCY

A four-time All-Star, Francis "King" Clancy was a crafty defender who was noted as much for his gift of gab on the ice as he was for his defensive abilities. He also served time behind the bench as a coach and in a striped shirt as a referee. In Game 4 of the 1923 Stanley Cup Finals while playing for the Ottawa Senators, Clancy played all six positions, including rover and goalie.

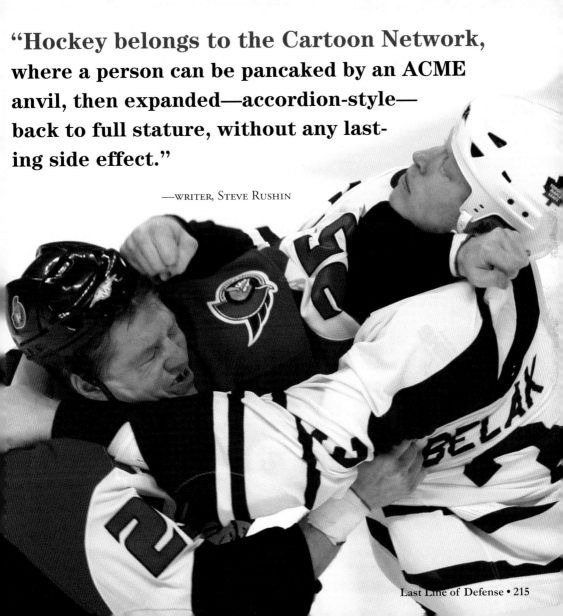

"Hockey belongs to the Cartoon Network, where a person can be pancaked by an ACME anvil, then expanded—accordion-style—back to full stature, without any lasting side effect."

—WRITER, STEVE RUSHIN

Hollywood Miracle

In the 2004 film *Miracle*, Kurt Russell stars as the enigmatic Herb Brooks in the cinematic tale of the *U.S. hockey team's stunning defeat of the Soviet Union at the 1980 Olympics.* Even though the story is well known and the outcome never in doubt, the film creates *tension, triumph, and relief.* Russell captures every nuance and contradiction of the resolute coach with sublime subtlety. Moreover, the on-ice action is portrayed with exceptional accuracy by a cast of nonactors who never fail to shoot and score.

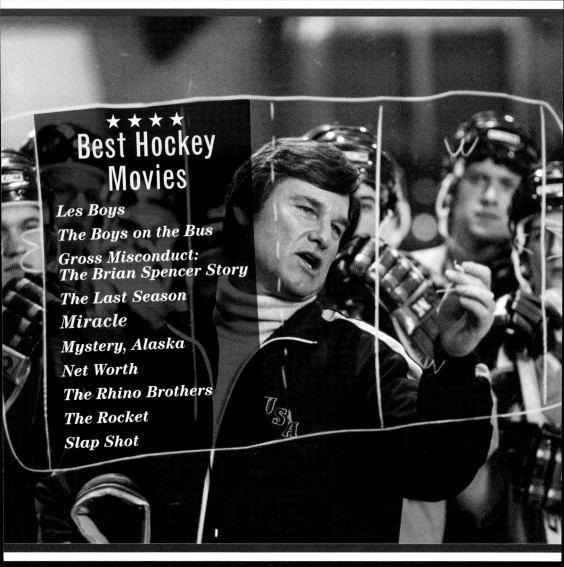

★ ★ ★ ★
Best Hockey Movies

Les Boys

The Boys on the Bus

*Gross Misconduct:
The Brian Spencer Story*

The Last Season

Miracle

Mystery, Alaska

Net Worth

The Rhino Brothers

The Rocket

Slap Shot

MOST CAREER SHUTOUTS

MARTIN BRODEUR..............125

TERRY SAWCHUK...............103

GEORGE HAINSWORTH.......94

GLENN HALL.......................84

JACQUES PLANTE...............82

DOMINIK HASEK.................81

TINY THOMPSON................81

ALEX CONNELL...................81

TONY ESPOSITO.................76

ED BELFOUR.......................76

Terry Sawchuk

Denis, Denis, Denis . . .

On February 4, 1961, three babies named Denis were born. This trio of tykes all grew up in the same neighborhood of Verdun, Quebec, sharing a passion for the game of hockey and a love of the Montreal Canadiens. Later, all three played together on the same line for the Montreal Jr. Canadiens, a team in the Quebec Major Junior Hockey League. Denis Savard went on to enjoy a Hall of Fame career, collecting 1,338 points in the NHL and having his number retired by the Chicago Blackhawks. Denis Cyr, a first-round draft selection of the Calgary Flames, also played for the Blackhawks. Denis Tremblay never made it to the NHL, but he did have a big-league audition——with the Blackhawks.

THE SITTLER SYSTEM

In one six-month span, Toronto Maple Leafs captain Darryl Sittler cemented his spot in hockey lore with three outstanding individual performances. In a game against Boston on February 7, 1976, Sittler collected six goals and 10 points, a single-game NHL record that remains untouched. In the playoffs against Philadelphia later that season, he became just the third player to score five goals in a postseason game. He topped off his marvelous run of productivity in September by scoring the overtime winner over Finland that delivered the Canada Cup to the host country.

Martin Brodeur

"Magic Marty"

Set an NHL record with 48 wins in 2006–07. Led the league in victories nine times from 1997–98 to 2006–07, reaching 40 wins a record eight times.

● ● ●

Became the youngest goalie in NHL history (age 29) to record 300 wins after whitewashing the Ottawa Senators on December 15, 2001.

● ● ●

Has won three Stanley Cup titles with New Jersey and two Olympic gold medals with Canada.

● ● ●

Set NHL records for career wins and shutouts.

NHL STATISTICS

REGULAR SEASON					PLAYOFFS				
W	L	T	SO	GAA	W	L	T	SO	GAA
688	394	154	124	2.24	113	91	0	24	2.02

A tireless perfectionist who excels under pressure, Brodeur was a throwback to the golden era of the game, when goalies showed up every night expecting to play.

AL MacINNIS

A roving rearguard and master-blaster whose slap shot was regularly clocked at more than 100 mph, Al MacInnis became the first defenseman to lead all skaters in playoff scoring when he captured the Conn Smythe Trophy with the Calgary Flames in 1989. MacInnis, who used his devastating shot to register seven 20-goal seasons, was named to the NHL's First All-Star Team four times. In 1998–99, he won the Norris Trophy as the league's top blue-liner.

Box Trot

1) Which Hall of Fame member was the last NHL coach to be suspended because of a bench-clearing brawl?

2) Who holds the record for most penalty minutes in a single period?

3) Who was the first player to reach 50 goals and 250 PIM in the same season?

4) Which gentlemanly player set a team record for points and penalty minutes in the same season?

5) What are the ingredients of a "Gordie Howe hat trick"?

6) Who holds the record for most penalties in a single game?

STANLEY CUP CLASSICS

ROCKET IN A POCKET

Raw rookie Ken Dryden starred in goal for the Montreal
Canadiens throughout the 1971 playoffs. Still, it was an aging
veteran who put the finishing touches on an unlikely run to
the Stanley Cup title. Coach Al MacNeil had actually benched
Henri Richard (*pictured, above Cup*) during the early stages
of the Finals versus Chicago, but the "Pocket Rocket" came
to the rescue in Game 7. Making like his big brother, Maurice,
Henri scored the tying and winning goals as the Canadiens
rallied from a 2–0 deficit to claim the Stanley Cup.

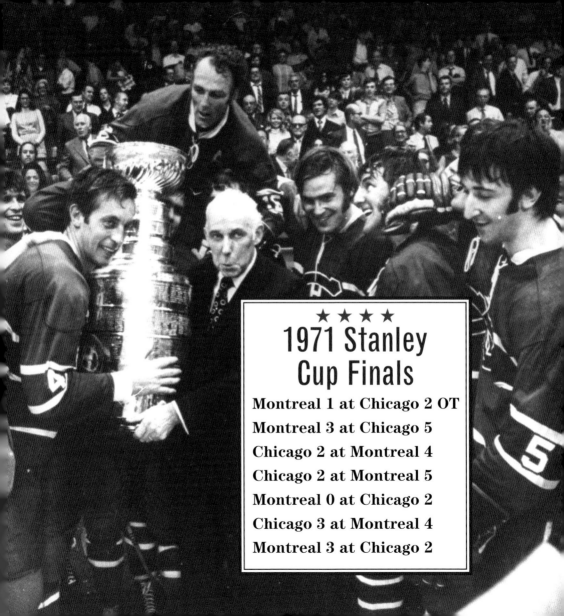

★ ★ ★ ★
1971 Stanley Cup Finals

Montreal 1 at Chicago 2 OT

Montreal 3 at Chicago 5

Chicago 2 at Montreal 4

Chicago 2 at Montreal 5

Montreal 0 at Chicago 2

Chicago 3 at Montreal 4

Montreal 3 at Chicago 2

One-Game Wonders

More than 300 players have suited up for only one game in the NHL. Some, such as goalie Danny Olesevich, were actually assistant trainers and practice goalies who were called into duty when the incumbent cage plumber was unable to continue because of injury. Two players, however, made the most out of the least. Rolly Huard, a journeyman forward in the Maple Leafs system, scored a goal in his only NHL game during the 1930–31 season. More recently, Brad Fast, a Carolina Hurricanes draft selection, scored a goal in his only claim to NHL fame in the 2003–04 campaign.

FACE OF HOCKEY

The Rangers had a bloody Mess on their hands during this game from 2002. It was only fitting that Mark Messier's blood matched the color of his captain's C, for he was always willing to spill it for the sake of the team.

Comeback Kids

If you're up 3-0 on Philadelphia, the Flyers have you right where they want you. At least they did in 2010.

The Boston Bruins won the first three games in the Eastern Conference semifinals that year, needing just one more victory to move on to the conference championship series. That victory never came. The scrappy Flyers scratched and clawed their way to three straight wins, setting up a winner-take-all seventh game.

There, they once again dug a 3-0 hole for themselves. This time it was on the first-period scoreboard. But a goal before the first intermission and two in the second period tied the game, and Simon Gagne lit the lamp on the power *play with 7:08 remaining to hoist Philadelphia to a series victory that defied logic. The Flyers became just the third team in NHL history to win a series after dropping the first three games.*

COMING BACK FROM 3 GAMES DOWN

Teams that have rallied from 3-0 deficits to win series in the Stanley Cup playoffs:

- 2010 Flyers (vs. Bruins)
- 1975 Islanders (vs. Penguins)
- 1942 Maple Leafs (vs. Red Wings)

Jacques Plante

"Jake the Snake"

Goaltender Jacques Plante was an innovator who understood the game as well as anyone ever to play it. Known respectfully as "Jake the Snake" due to his outstanding mobility, Plante was the first goalie to routinely leave his crease area to handle and pass the puck. In a career that spanned 18 NHL seasons, Plante won six Stanley Cups with the Canadiens and seven Vezina Trophies.

Growing up on a farm in Quebec, Plante was the oldest of 11 children. He became a goalie during his youth career only after an asthmatic condition curtailed his skating ability. He was a natural between the pipes and soon caught the attention of the Habs, who brought him to the NHL as a starter in 1954–55, two years after he had helped them win the 1952–53 Stanley Cup. In 1954–55, his first full season, he led the NHL in wins (31). The following year, he won a career-high 42 games and took the goals-against title (1.86) en route to his first Vezina Trophy. He then carried the Canadiens to the first of five consecutive Stanley Cups.

In 1956–57, Jake the Snake won his second of five straight Vezina Trophies when he finished the season with a 2.02 GAA, which he lowered to 1.75 in the playoffs as Montreal skated past the Rangers and Boston to win another title. The Habs repeated as playoff champs in 1957–58 and 1958–59, with Plante winning Vezinas each season.

Struck in the face by a slap shot early in the 1959–60 campaign, Plante responded by wearing a mask, becoming the first goalie ever to do so on a regular basis. Any fears that it would curtail his ability were erased when he led the Canadiens to another Stanley Cup in the spring of 1960, with a 1.35 playoff GAA. In 1961–62, Plante won 42 games for the second time in his career. He captured the Hart Trophy and the Vezina Trophy, becoming the first goalie ever to win both awards in a single season.

Plante toiled for the Rangers from 1963 to '65, then came out of retirement to play for the St. Louis Blues from 1968 to '70. He suited up for Toronto and Boston before ending his NHL career in 1973. He retired with 434 wins—second most, at the time, in NHL history.

NHL STATISTICS

REGULAR SEASON					PLAYOFFS				
W	L	T	SO	GAA	W	L	T	SO	GAA
434	247	146	82	2.38	71	37	0	14	2.16

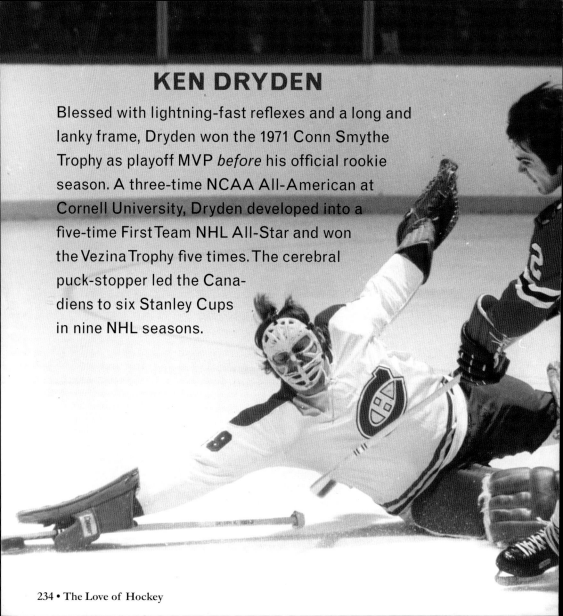

KEN DRYDEN

Blessed with lightning-fast reflexes and a long and lanky frame, Dryden won the 1971 Conn Smythe Trophy as playoff MVP *before* his official rookie season. A three-time NCAA All-American at Cornell University, Dryden developed into a five-time First Team NHL All-Star and won the Vezina Trophy five times. The cerebral puck-stopper led the Canadiens to six Stanley Cups in nine NHL seasons.

What's My Line?

This Philadelphia Flyers trio seems pleasant enough, but on the ice they terrorized opposing goalies. In fact, this line of Reggie Leach, Bobby Clarke, and Bill Barber (*left to right*) combined for 141 goals in 1975–76 while propelling the Flyers to their third straight Stanley Cup Finals. What was their line called?

THE MADHOUSE ON MADISON

When it opened in 1929 (and for many years afterward), Chicago Stadium was the largest indoor arena in the world. It was capable of holding 25,000 people, and though it officially sat 17,317 for hockey, standing-room-only fans regularly swelled the crowd to 18,500. Crowds dipped much lower than that during the 1940s and '50s, but Bobby Hull brought them back, and the Blackhawks became a powerhouse during the 1960s. Chicago Stadium was known for its loud crowds, but what really gave the Stadium its Madhouse atmosphere was the fabled 3,663-pipe Barton organ.

TALES OF THE
STANLEY CUP

ERRORS IN COMMISSION

Since the engraving of the Stanley Cup is painstakingly done by hand, there is bound to be the odd error in spelling and accuracy. Careful examination of the etched globe reveals that clubs such as the New York "Ilanders," the Toronto Maple "Leaes," and the "Bqstqn" Bruins have all won the Cup. Fictitious names, such as Alex "Belvecchio," "Gave" Stewart, and Tommy "Nivan," are credited on the Cup at the expense of the actual players and coaches. Jacques Plante's name is misspelled five times, and Hal Winkler is on the Cup as a member of the Boston Bruins in 1929—even though he never played a game with the team that season.

SABRETOOTH

An acrobatic and athletic beast,
Sabretooth parades around
the entire confines of Buffalo's
HSBC Arena shooting T-shirts
into the air. Sabretooth likes to
bill himself as the league's only
left-handed mascot. He is also a
two-sport star, as he originally
plied his manic mannerisms for
the Buffalo Bandits, the city's
indoor lacrosse franchise.

Baun Guts It Out

Known as a bruising, stay-at-home defenseman, Toronto's Bob Baun was equally renowned for his ability to play through pain. He accented that reputation during Game 6 of the 1964 Stanley Cup Finals between the Red Wings and Maple Leafs. Baun took a Gordie Howe slap shot off the ankle and left the ice on a stretcher. Remarkably, he returned in time for overtime. Early in OT, the burly blue-liner flipped a shot that hopped, skipped, and somehow jumped past goaltender Terry Sawchuk. After the Leafs dispatched the Wings to win the Cup in Game 7, it was revealed that Baun had tallied his memorable marker while playing on a heavily taped, and badly broken, ankle.

Bob Baun

Holey Goalie

During World War II, the NHL encouraged players to enlist in the armed services——and they did so by the dozens. In fact, entering training camp in 1942, the New York Rangers found themselves without a single netminder. "Find me a goalie," cried Rangers manager Lester Patrick. "Any goalie!" They found one in Swift Current, Saskatchewan. Steve Buzinski was full of confidence but, it turned out, short on talent. In his nine-game career with the Rangers, he posted an abysmal 6.11 goals-against average. In one game, he accidentally tossed the puck into his own net! He was forevermore known as Steve Buzinski "The Puck Goesinski."

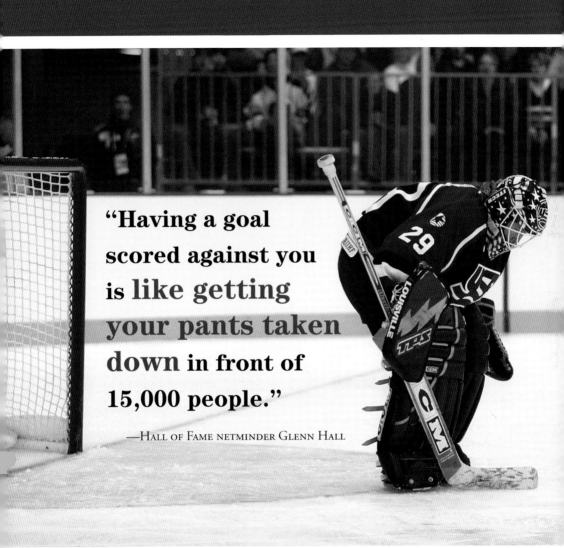

"Having a goal scored against you is like getting your pants taken down in front of 15,000 people."

—Hall of Fame netminder Glenn Hall

Ever the Gentleman

For as rough and rugged as hockey can be, the NHL annually honors one of its standouts for — of all things — being gentlemanly. The Lady Byng Memorial Trophy is one of the most prestigious in the game, awarded to the player "adjudged to have exhibited the best type of sportsmanship and gentlemanly conduct combined with a high standard of playing ability."

Three times since 2010, that high honor went to Martin St. Louis of the Tampa Bay Lightning. St. Louis, an undersized sparkplug who led the Lightning to their first Stanley Cup title in 2004, was a class act on and off the ice, endearing himself to everyone but the opposing goaltender.

ST. LOUIS STATISTICS

GP	G	A	PTS	PIM
1,134	391	642	1033	310

Haunted by personal demons and riddled by a litany of injuries throughout his career, Sawchuk nonetheless became the NHL's all-time leader in wins and shutouts. He died in 1970 at age 40 following an alcohol-induced fight with New York Rangers teammate Ron Stewart.

Terry Sawchuk

"Uke"

Was the winning goalie in all eight games of the 1952 playoffs for Detroit. Won four of them by shutout, and didn't allow a single goal on home ice.

● ● ●

Won the Vezina Trophy three times with the Red Wings and shared the award in 1964–65 with Johnny Bower in Toronto.

● ● ●

Recorded at least 40 wins in a season three times and was named to the NHL First or Second All-Star Team seven times.

● ● ●

Was the first goalie to be elected to Hockey Hall of Fame without having to serve the three-year waiting period.

NHL STATISTICS

REGULAR SEASON					PLAYOFFS				
W	L	T	SO	GAA	W	L	T	SO	GAA
447	330	172	103	2.52	54	48	0	12	2.54

GLENN HALL

Nicknamed "Mr. Goalie" during his 19-year NHL career, Hall was the innovator and first practitioner of the butterfly technique of goaltending. He was named the NHL's rookie of the year with Detroit in 1955–56, and he earned the Conn Smythe Trophy as playoff MVP with St. Louis in 1968. Hall, who led the league in shutouts six times with three different teams, established a record that will never be broken: He appeared in 502 consecutive games as a bare-faced goaltender.

HALL OF FAME TREASURES

Left: *Many NHL players skated for service teams during World War II. Pictured is a jersey for a Royal Canadian Air Force team, which was appropriately named the Flyers.* Right: *The New York Americans survived as an NHL franchise from 1925 to 1942, sharing Madison Square Garden with the New York Rangers. However, the team enjoyed only three winning seasons. Troubled times during the Depression and World War II led to its demise.*

Beaver and His Brother

When he retired following the 1988—89 season, Marcel Dionne had only one blemish on his Hall of Fame career. Despite pounding 731 pucks past enemy goaltenders and collecting 1,771 points, "Little Beaver" never had the opportunity to sip champagne from Lord Stanley's majestic mug. In fact, Dionne had never even appeared in the Stanley Cup Finals during his 18 NHL seasons. In an ironic twist of fate, his baby brother, Gilbert, who was 19 years younger than Dionne, won the Stanley Cup in only his third NHL season as a member of the 1992—93 Canadiens. Marcel described watching his brother raise the Cup above his head as the proudest moment of his hockey career.

Canadiens fans enjoy their "guy" time during a road trip to Vancouver in January 2006. Despite these men's desire to keep "wives at home," a reported 41 percent of NHL spectators are women—the highest figure among the four major team sports.

HERE'S HOWES

When Gordie Howe decided to end his retirement and sign with the upstart Houston Aeros, it afforded him the opportunity to play with his sons, Mark and Marty, both of whom had been inked to contracts by the WHA club. After four productive campaigns in Texas, the first family of hockey moved on to New England. When the Whalers joined the NHL for the 1979–80 season, Gordie and boys made the journey with them. That season, the 51-year-old grandfather became the first and only player to start an NHL game on the same forward line as his sons.

George Hainsworth

SHUTOUTS IN A SEASON

22	GEORGE HAINSWORTH, MON	1928–29		13	ALEX CONNELL, OTT	1926–27
15	ALEX CONNELL, OTT	1925–26		13	GEORGE HAINSWORTH, MON	1927–28
15	ALEX CONNELL, OTT	1927–28		13	JOHN ROSS ROACH, NYR	1928–29
15	HAL WINKLER, BOS	1927–28		13	ROY WORTERS, NYA	1928–29
15	TONY ESPOSITO, CHI	1969–70		13	HARRY LUMLEY, TOR	1953–54
14	GEORGE HAINSWORTH, MON	1926–27		13	DOMINIK HASEK, BUF	1997–98
13	CLINT BENEDICT, MAROONS	1926–27				

Avalanche superstar Joe Sakic didn't have to sneak a peek into the Stanley Cup crate to view the fabled mug, as he's doing in this 2006 promotional shoot. Sakic was personally presented with the Cup in 1996 and 2001 after Colorado prevailed in the Stanley Cup Finals.

STANLEY CUP

FRAGILE

FRAGILE

NHL

One Short of Two Dozen

For 82 years, the Boston Bruins were the only team in NHL history to boast 22 consecutive home wins — a record that lasted more than eight decades! That's how impressive the Detroit Red Wings were from November 3, 2011 to February 19, 2012, when they rattled off 23 straight wins at Joe Louis Arena to break one of the longest-standing marks in sports.

The clinching triumph could hardly have come against a better opponent. San Jose had won five consecutive regular-season games over Detroit. The Sharks were also the team that eliminated the Red Wings in each of the previous two postseasons. This time, backup goalie Joey MacDonald sparked streaking Detroit with 31 saves in a 3-2 victory.

The Red Wings then lost their next two home games — a mere footnote under one of the best streaks in sports.

Russell Williams, a *long*-time Senators fan, attends Game 3 of the 2007 Stanley Cup Finals between Ottawa and the Anaheim Ducks. Williams was in attendance when the original Senators won the Cup in 1927.

BRIAN LEETCH

The only native of Texas to become an NHL All-Star, Brian Leetch was a gifted playmaker and the last defenseman to record 100 points in a season. Leetch, who quarterbacked the power play and anchored the defense, was a cerebral player who could anticipate a play before it occurred. In 1994, he won the Conn Smythe Trophy when he helped the Rangers escort Lord Stanley back to Broadway.

Barilko's goal

STANLEY CUP CLASSICS
THE ALL-OVERTIME FINALS

The 1951 Stanley Cup Finals would have been memorable anyway. With every game going into overtime, this battle between rival cities was a classic despite lasting only five games. Yet the saga of the season's Stanley Cup hero elevates this series to mythic status. Early in overtime of Game 5, Toronto defenseman Bill Barilko charged in from the blue line and chopped a shot past Montreal goalie Gerry McNeil. Later that summer, Barilko disappeared while on a fishing trip. The Leafs did not win the Cup again until 1962—the year that Barilko's remains and the plane that carried him to his demise were finally discovered.

★ ★ ★ ★
1951 Stanley Cup Finals

Montreal 2 at Toronto 3 OT
Montreal 3 at Toronto 2 OT
Toronto 2 at Montreal 1 OT
Toronto 3 at Montreal 2 OT
Montreal 2 at Toronto 3 OT

CHAPTER SIX

BACK OF THE NET

"Every time a puck gets past me and I look back into the net, I say, 'Uh-oh.'"

—BERNIE PARENT

Jaromir Jagr

"The Jaguar"

Was named to the NHL First All-Star Team seven times, won
the Hart Trophy in 1998–99, captured five Art Ross
Trophies, and won a pair of Stanley Cup titles with Pittsburgh
(1990–91 and 1991–92).

● ● ●

Scored more points than any European-born player
in NHL history.

● ● ●

Scored at least 30 goals in 15 consecutive seasons, and holds
the NHL record for most points by a right winger in a single
campaign (149).

● ● ●

Established eight team records in his first season with the
Rangers (2005–06), including most points (123) and goals (54).

NHL STATISTICS

REGULAR SEASON					PLAYOFFS				
GP	G	A	PTS	PIM	GP	G	A	PTS	PIM
1,692	749	1,119	1,868	1,101	202	78	121	199	159

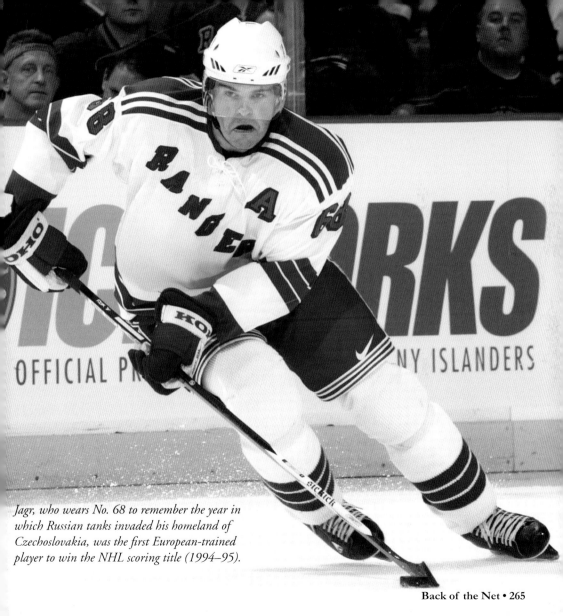

Jagr, who wears No. 68 to remember the year in which Russian tanks invaded his homeland of Czechoslovakia, was the first European-trained player to win the NHL scoring title (1994–95).

Seeing Double

On September 26, 1980, in a Swedish town of less than 30,000 residents, NHL scoring championships were born to Tommy and Tora Sedin. Their names: Henrik and Daniel, identical and inseparable twin brothers who would share a gift for putting pucks in the net.

Teammates with the Vancouver Canucks since 2000 and on several Swedish national teams over the years, the Sedins pose double-trouble for opponents. In addition to being, individually, among the most skilled players in the game, together they are almost unstoppable. Their years of playing together and uncanny biological connection are almost unfair.

Henrik won the Art Ross Trophy as the NHL's top point-getter in 2009-10; Daniel earned it the following season. Together, they led Sweden to the 2006 Olympic gold medal.

SEDIN REGULAR-SEASON STATS

HENRIK

GP	G	A	PTS	PIM
1,166	222	748	970	622

DANIEL

GP	G	A	PTS	PIM
1,143	355	587	942	474

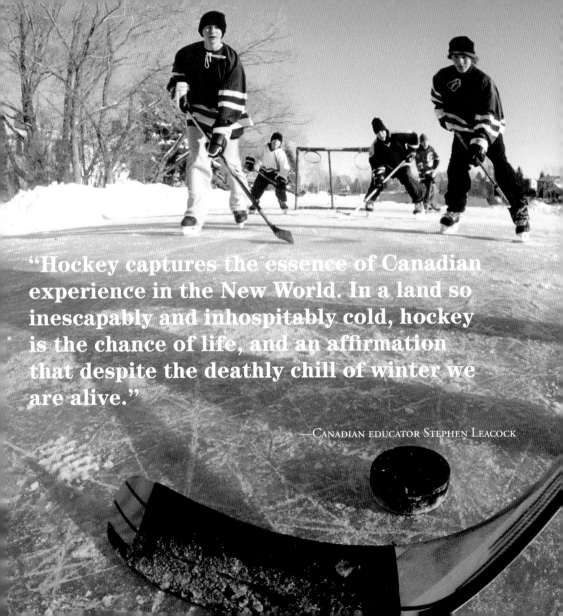

"Hockey captures the essence of Canadian experience in the New World. In a land so inescapably and inhospitably cold, hockey is the chance of life, and an affirmation that despite the deathly chill of winter we are alive."

—CANADIAN EDUCATOR STEPHEN LEACOCK

NIGHTS ON BROADWAY

Located in the heart of Manhattan on Seventh Avenue between 31st and 33rd streets, Madison Square Garden is known as the World's Most Famous Arena. Ninety-four years after the original MSG was built, the current Madison Square Garden was unveiled in 1968. The opening of the newest Garden coincided with the return to glory of the New York Rangers after a dismal stretch that saw the team miss the playoffs 18 times in 25 years. Still, it took until 1994 before the new Garden's faithful celebrated a Stanley Cup triumph—the team's first since 1940.

FANTASTIC FANS

The two Calgary fans on the right thought they were Cup crazy until they ran into the guy on the left. All were headed to the Saddledome to watch the Flames host Tampa Bay in Game 3 of the 2004 Stanley Cup Finals.

The Art of Ross

Art Ross was not only one of the finest rearguards to play the game, he was also one of hockey's greatest innovators, architects, and managers. Ross designed the modern goal net, which is still in use today; introduced the smooth-edged or "beveled" puck to the sport; initiated the first system for compiling plus/minus statistics; and served as an NHL referee. As the first general manager and coach of the Boston Bruins, he helped name the club, design the logo, build the franchise, and guide the team into the Stanley Cup winner's circle three times before retiring in 1954.

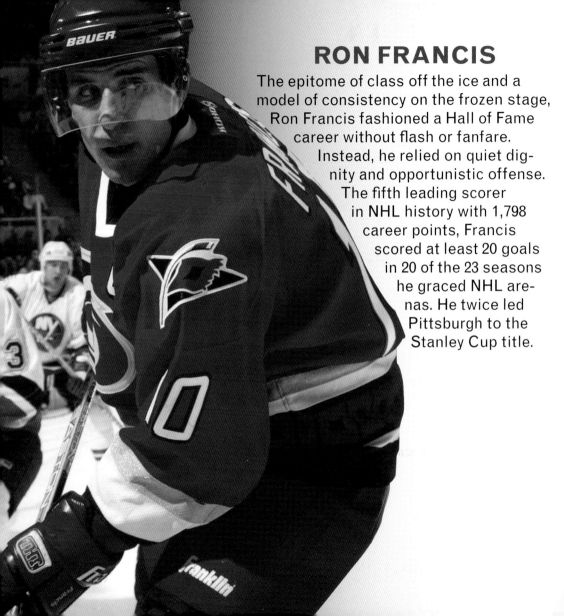

RON FRANCIS

The epitome of class off the ice and a model of consistency on the frozen stage, Ron Francis fashioned a Hall of Fame career without flash or fanfare. Instead, he relied on quiet dignity and opportunistic offense. The fifth leading scorer in NHL history with 1,798 career points, Francis scored at least 20 goals in 20 of the 23 seasons he graced NHL arenas. He twice led Pittsburgh to the Stanley Cup title.

Living in Sin

Until the start of the 1965—66 season, it was common practice for NHL combatants to bash and crash each other on the ice, get flagged by the referee for their transgressions, and then serve their penance sitting together in the same penalty box. Suffice it to say that on more than one occasion the feuding pugilists did more than exchange pleasantries while pontificating on the pine. Still, most owners were not pleased when the NHL passed legislation requiring all arenas to have two separate penalty benches. The extended penalty box areas eliminated some of the top revenue-generating seats in the rink.

Heavyweight Title Bout

On December 2, 1992, at Madison Square Garden, Rangers hitman Tie Domi and Detroit tough guy Bob Probert engaged in a rematch of an earlier bout in which *Domi had bloodied the Red Wing's nose.* Thanks to Domi's brash pre-bout jaw-flapping, fans knew a marquee rematch was about to unfold.

One witness counted *60 punches thrown,* with Probert narrowly declared the winner—and still heavyweight champion.

★ ★ ★ ★
Ugliest Fights

Henry Boucha vs. Dave Forbes, 1/4/75
Canadiens vs. Nordiques, 4/20/84
Ted Green vs. Wayne Maki, 9/21/69
Gordie Howe vs. Lou Fontinato, 2/1/59
Joey Kocur vs. Brad Dalgarno, 2/21/89
Bob Probert vs. Tie Domi, 12/2/92
Maurice Richard vs. Hal Laycoe, 3/13/55
Patrick Roy vs. Mike Vernon, 3/26/97
Dave Schultz vs. Dale Rolfe, 5/5/74
Eddie Shack vs. Larry Zeidel, 3/7/68

MAGICAL MOMENTS

THIS FLIGHT TONIGHT

Bobby Orr, the offensive catalyst of the Boston Bruins, entered Game 4 of the 1970 Stanley Cup Finals against St. Louis without a goal in the championship round. But early in the first overtime session, Orr corralled the puck in his own zone and sped up the ice in one of his patented rushes. After cruising into the Blues' zone, he threw a feed to Derek Sanderson, who delivered a perfect give-and-go pass that Orr deftly deflected past Blues goaltender Glenn Hall for the series-winning tally. As the puck smacked the net, Orr soared through the air with his arms extended in a midflight celebration.

Gordie Howe and Ted Lindsay toil in the workshop of Howe's basement on February 16, 1951. Two-thirds of Detroit's Production Line, Howe and Lindsay each made the NHL First All-Star Team in 1950–51.

CANDID CAMERA

LEGENDARY LASTS

1) Who was the last Hall of Fame goalie to play without a mask?

2) Who was the last player from the Original Six era to retire?

3) Who was the last NHLer to play without a helmet?

4) Who was the last player to score back-to-back overtime goals in the Stanley Cup Finals?

5) Who was the last goaltender to serve as a captain of an NHL team?

6) Who was the last player to play in both the WHA *and* the NHL?

Answers: 1) Gump Worsley, 1973–74; 2) Wayne Cashman, 1982–83; 3) Craig MacTavish, 1996–97; 4) John LeClair, 1993; 5) Bill Durnan, 1947–48; 6) Mark Messier, 2003–04

Hall of Fame Treasures

Below: *In the early days of the NHL, referees used bells in place of whistles. These belonged to legendary ref Bobby Hewitson.* Right: *Frank Udvari became the supervisor of NHL officials in the mid-1960s. He was honored with this unique trophy in 1966.*

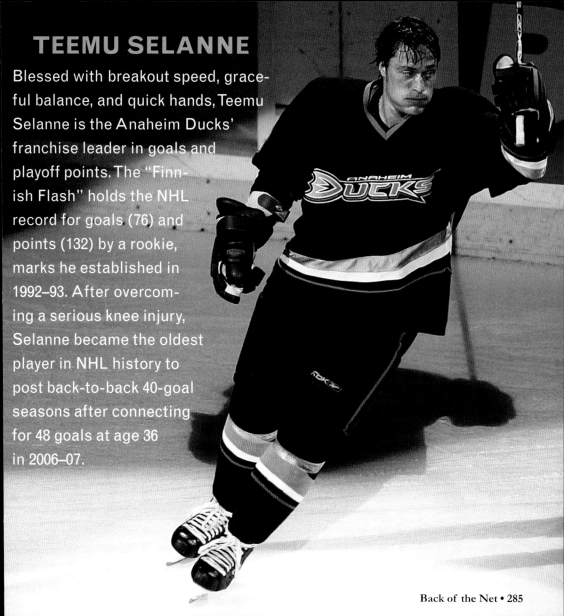

TEEMU SELANNE

Blessed with breakout speed, grace-ful balance, and quick hands, Teemu Selanne is the Anaheim Ducks' franchise leader in goals and playoff points. The "Finn-ish Flash" holds the NHL record for goals (76) and points (132) by a rookie, marks he established in 1992–93. After overcom-ing a serious knee injury, Selanne became the oldest player in NHL history to post back-to-back 40-goal seasons after connecting for 48 goals at age 36 in 2006–07.

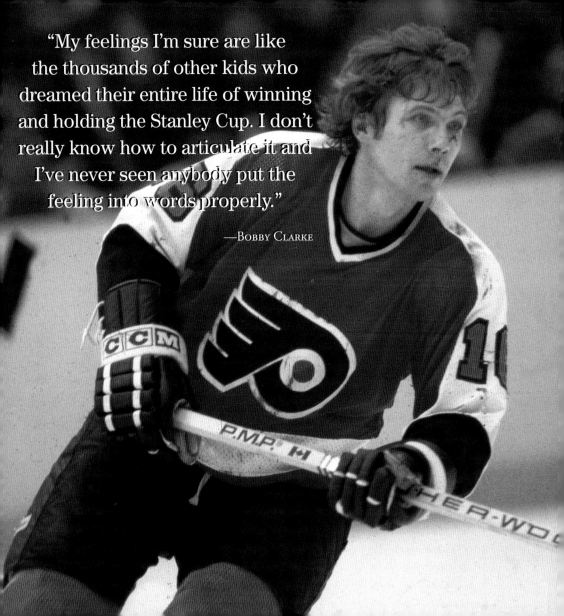

"My feelings I'm sure are like the thousands of other kids who dreamed their entire life of winning and holding the Stanley Cup. I don't really know how to articulate it and I've never seen anybody put the feeling into words properly."

—Bobby Clarke

Bobby Clarke

"Captain Courageous"

The heart and soul of the Flyers, Clarke overcame diabetes to record three 100-point seasons and lead the Flyers to the Stanley Cup championship in 1973–74 and 1974–75.

● ● ●

Won the Hart Trophy in 1972–73, 1974–75, and 1975–76. Also captured the Masterton Trophy in 1971–72 and the Selke Trophy in 1982–83.

● ● ●

Played in eight NHL All-Star Games and twice led the league in assists.

● ● ●

Guided both the Minnesota North Stars (1991–92) and the Flyers (1996–97) to the Stanley Cup Finals as a general manager.

NHL STATISTICS

REGULAR SEASON					PLAYOFFS				
GP	G	A	PTS	PIM	GP	G	A	PTS	PIM
1,144	358	852	1,210	1,453	136	42	77	119	152

What's My Line?

In 1929, Maple Leafs coach Conn Smythe put 23-year-old Joe Primeau (*middle*) on a line with a pair of 18-year-olds—Charlie Conacher (*left*) and Harvey "Busher" Jackson (*right*). Together, they led Toronto to a Stanley Cup title in 1932 and four Stanley Cup Finals appearances over the following six years. What was the name of this line?

Answer: The Kid Line

A Foot Note

The first Russian-born player to skate in the NHL was Val Hoffinger, who entered the world in Seltz, Russia, but was raised in Salvador, Saskatchewan. A star defenseman with the Saskatoon Sheiks of the Western Hockey League, Hoffinger made his NHL debut with the Chicago Black Hawks in 1927–28. After retiring, he coached the German Olympic team in the 1936 Olympics—which earned him an audience with Chancellor Adolf Hitler—and went on to become a world-renowned podiatrist. Hoffinger married Bernice Scholl, the daughter of Dr. William Scholl, the famous orthopedic foot-product manufacturer.

STANLEY CUP CLASSICS

LESWICK'S LUCK

With Detroit ahead three games to one and Jacques Plante fighting the puck in the Canadiens goal, Montreal coach Dick Irvin turned to Gerry McNeil for Game 5 of the 1954 Stanley Cup Finals. He kept the Canadiens alive with a 1–0 shutout victory. The Habs followed with a 4–1 win in Game 6, but their luck was exhausted by Game 7. With the scored tied 1–1 early in overtime, Tony Leswick lofted the puck toward the Montreal net. Defenseman Doug Harvey reached up to grab it, but the puck deflected off his glove and over McNeil's shoulder. Leswick's lucky goal gave Detroit the Stanley Cup in the last Game 7 to require extra time.

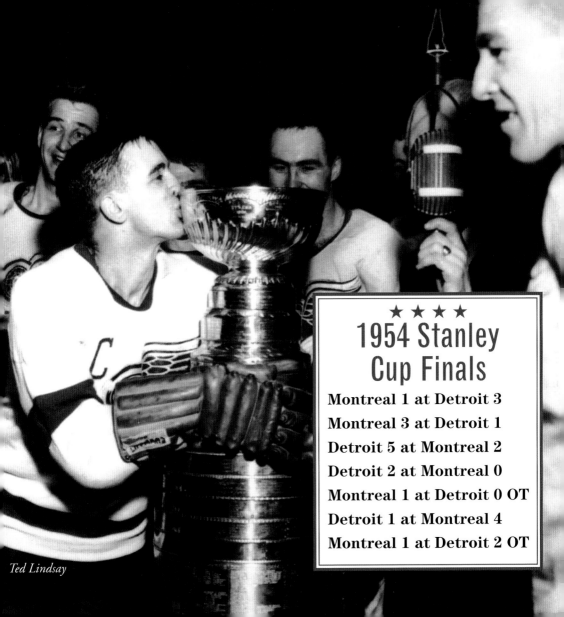

★ ★ ★ ★
1954 Stanley Cup Finals

Montreal 1 at Detroit 3
Montreal 3 at Detroit 1
Detroit 5 at Montreal 2
Detroit 2 at Montreal 0
Montreal 1 at Detroit 0 OT
Detroit 1 at Montreal 4
Montreal 1 at Detroit 2 OT

Ted Lindsay

One-Man Club

Hockey's "Triple Gold Club" consists of those who have captured three coveted awards — the Stanley Cup, the World Championship and an Olympic gold medal. More than two dozen players have gained membership, but only one coach in history has done so.

Mike Babcock, who in 2015 signed a record $50 million contract to coach the Toronto Maple Leafs, became the Triple Gold Club's lone boss when he led Team Canada to a gold medal in the 2010 Olympic Games on home soil in Vancouver. He accomplished the World Championship leg of the "Triple" back in 2004 and led the Red Wings to the Cup in '08. For good measure (and a heaping dose of national pride), Babcock added a second Olympic gold in '14.

In recognition of the Triple Gold Club feat, Saskatoon, Saskatchewan — the town he grew up in — named July 17, 2010 "Mike Babcock Day."

BABCOCK BITS:

• Led the Mighty Ducks of Anaheim to the 2003 Stanley Cup final.

• In 10 years at the Red Wings helm, won five division titles and the 2008 Cup, and made another appearance in the Cup finals in '09.

• He and legendary former Soviet coach Viktor Tikhonov are the only men to lead their teams to back-to-back Olympic gold medals.

From Rollerblades to the Big Stage

Joe Mullen grew up in the concrete jungle of Hell's Kitchen in the heart of New York City, where seemingly the only available ice was found in the drinks of neighborhood taverns. Mullen began playing hockey by wearing Rollerblades on the paved streets of the Big Apple. He didn't slip his feet into a pair of ice skates until he was 10 years old. Despite those restrictions, he earned a scholarship to Boston College and molded himself into a gritty, tenacious forward who became the first American-born player to score 500 goals and register 1,000 points—totals that earned him a berth in the Hockey Hall of Fame.

FACE OF HOCKEY

Two young fans flash southern smiles during a 2003–04 battle between the Atlanta Thrashers and Florida Panthers at Philips Arena in Atlanta.

The Goalie Shoots . . . He Scores!

Ron Hextall, a longtime Philadelphia Flyers goalie, wasn't afraid to use his stick. When he wasn't wandering outside his crease to handle the rubber, he was whacking opponents who crowded his territory. On December 8, 1987, Hextall used his lumber to score a goal—the first ever tallied by an NHL netminder. With the Flyers up by two, the Boston Bruins pulled their goalie late in the game, giving Hextall an easy target. Amazingly, Hextall repeated the feat the next season. He became the first NHL puck-stopper to net a playoff goal when he victimized the Washington Capitals on April 11, 1989.

Dave Andreychuk

MOST GAMES IN A CAREER

GORDIE HOWE	1,767
MARK MESSIER	1,756
RON FRANCIS	1,731
MARK RECCHI	1,652
CHRIS CHELIOS	1,651
DAVE ANDREYCHUK	1,639
SCOTT STEVENS	1,635
JAROMIR JAGR	1,629
LARRY MURPHY	1,615
RAY BOURQUE	1,612

Lacrosse-style Shooting

The move is almost commonplace now, but at the time no one had seen anything like it. In the NCAA regional final between Michigan and Minnesota on March 24, 1995, Wolverines forward Mike Legg grabbed a loose puck behind the Minnesota net. He scooped the disk up in the crease of his curve and, cradling the puck like a lacrosse ball, stepped around the rim of the crease and fired it past the bewildered Golden Gophers goalkeeper. Since then, both Pavel Bure and Sidney Crosby have exhibited their expertise at on-ice lacrosse, but it was Mike who got the first Legg up.

Record Smashing

"The Big Chill at the Big House" did not live up to its name on the thermometer, with temperatures in the 40s when the puck dropped. It did, however, coax plenty of goosebumps — not to mention a world record for hockey attendance. The announced crowd for the Michigan-Michigan State hockey game at Michigan Stadium on December 11, 2010, was 113,411. The official, certified attendance count was later deemed to be 104,173. The difference hardly mattered, as the previous record was less than 80,000 for a World Championship final in Germany.

On a rink stretching from one 15-yard line to the other in the "Big House," where Michigan typically smashes helmets with opposing football teams, the Wolverines shut out the Spartans by a 5-0 score. "We all got goosebumps," Michigan forward Carl Hagelin said. "It was just amazing to see all those people — probably the loudest environment I've ever been in."

Mark Messier

"Moose"

Measured against the greatest centers in NHL history, Mark Messier will always face comparison with longtime friend and teammate Wayne Gretzky, with whom he shared four Stanley Cup titles in Edmonton. Messier not only captained the Oilers to a fifth playoff title after No. 99 departed in 1988, but he then guided the 1993–94 Rangers to their first Stanley Cup in 54 years. He became the first man ever to captain two different teams to championships.

A native of Edmonton, Messier made his NHL debut with the Oilers in 1979–80 following an uneventful year in the WHA. He grew quickly into his role as second-line center behind Gretzky, and in his third season (1981–82) he finished with 50 goals.

Messier evolved into the backbone of the Oilers, the spiritual guide and jungle-tempered squad sergeant. In 1983–84, Edmonton knocked off the four-time defending champion New York Islanders to capture its first playoff title. Even in Gretzky's huge shadow, Messier's performance shone through, and he was voted the Conn Smythe Trophy.

The Oilers went through a brief rebuilding period in the immediate wake of Gretzky's exit, and Messier struggled with knee injuries that many feared would shorten his career. But he showed his trademark intensity and courage and regained both his health and his All-Star form. In 1989–90, he logged 45 goals and a career-high 129 points and won the Hart Trophy. Moreover, he took the Oilers to their fifth Stanley Cup in seven years. In the playoffs, he led all players with 22 assists.

In 1991–92, Messier went to Broadway and faced his biggest challenge: ending the longest Stanley Cup drought in NHL history. Mess was an instant smash. Not only did he lead the Rangers to the league's best record, but he notched his sixth 100-point season and was awarded a second Hart Trophy. In 1993–94, his dramatic Game 6 hat trick against the Devils allowed New York to play a seventh game, which the Rangers won in sudden-death. With Messier at the front, New York defeated Vancouver in the 1994 Cup Finals.

Messier played three more seasons with New York, three with Vancouver, and four more with the Rangers. When he retired in 2005, he ranked second in NHL history in both games played and career points.

NHL STATISTICS

REGULAR SEASON					PLAYOFFS				
GP	G	A	PTS	PIM	GP	G	A	PTS	PIM
1,756	694	1,193	1,887	1,910	236	109	186	295	244

The Net Cam

Calgary defenseman Mark Giordano (*right*) displays superhuman powers against Vancouver on April 8, 2006. Giordano prevents the puck from reaching the goal crease while simultaneously eliminating the Canucks' Richard Park as a possible threat.

S. J. SHARKIE

The first NHL mascot to have his own official Web site, S. J. has been swimming with the San Jose Sharks since 1992. Dubbed the "hardest working fish in show business," Sharkie appears at more than 350 events a year. He is a vocal advocate for the "Reading is Cool" literacy program, and he has appeared on both the silver screen and television.

Stan Mikita

"Czech Mate"

Played 22 seasons with Chicago and had his number (21) retired by the team after he hung up his skates in 1981.

● ● ●

Was the first player in NHL history to win three major trophies (Hart, Art Ross, and Lady Byng) in a single season, a feat he accomplished twice (1966–67 and 1967–68).

● ● ●

Known for his aggressive, combative style early in his career, he transformed himself into a graceful, gentlemanly player. Went from 154 PIM in 1964–65 to only 12 PIM in 1966–67.

● ● ●

Won the Art Ross Trophy four times and was named to the NHL First All-Star Team six times.

NHL STATISTICS

REGULAR SEASON					PLAYOFFS				
GP	G	A	PTS	PIM	GP	G	A	PTS	PIM
1,394	541	926	1,467	1,270	155	59	91	150	169

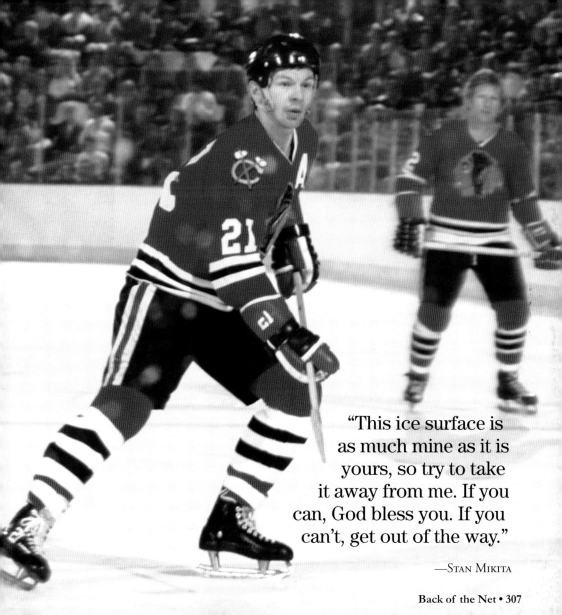

"This ice surface is as much mine as it is yours, so try to take it away from me. If you can, God bless you. If you can't, get out of the way."

—STAN MIKITA

ROCKY MOUNTAIN HIGH

Denver had a 40-year history of professional hockey when the Quebec Nordiques became the Colorado Avalanche on July 1, 1995. Within two months, 12,000 season tickets were sold. When the Avalanche won the Stanley Cup in June 1996, the love affair was official and the fans just kept on coming. In 1999, the Avalanche moved into the Pepsi Center, and in 2001 they celebrated a second Stanley Cup championship. Capacity crowds of 18,007 filled the arena every night, continuing a sellout streak that stretched to 487 consecutive games over 11 years.

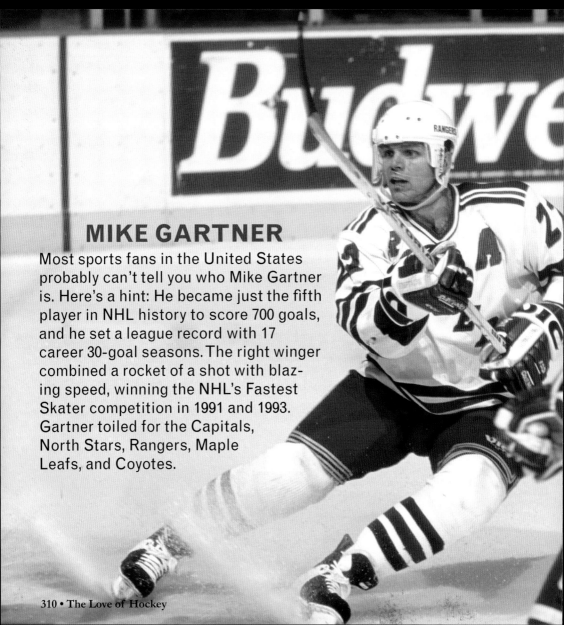

MIKE GARTNER

Most sports fans in the United States probably can't tell you who Mike Gartner is. Here's a hint: He became just the fifth player in NHL history to score 700 goals, and he set a league record with 17 career 30-goal seasons. The right winger combined a rocket of a shot with blazing speed, winning the NHL's Fastest Skater competition in 1991 and 1993. Gartner toiled for the Capitals, North Stars, Rangers, Maple Leafs, and Coyotes.

"Goaltenders are three sandwiches shy of a picnic."

—Journalist Jim Taylor

Baby, It's Cold Outside

Bundling up, hauling your skates and stick down to the local outdoor rink and slapping the puck around until mom calls you home (or when the streetlights come on, if that was the rule) is a tradition countless hockey players recall from their childhood days. The NHL, in 2008, made those memories part of its schedule.

The NHL Winter Classic pits two teams against one another in an outdoor venue — usually a football or baseball stadium in or near one of the cities — around the New Year's holiday. It has fast become one of the most popular games on the schedule, complete (in good years) with chilly air and falling snowflakes.

"It's one of those things you will remember for the rest of your life," Montreal defenseman P.K. Subban said after a win over Boston in Gillette Stadium in the 2016 version of the Classic.

WINTER CLASSIC RESULTS

2008: Pittsburgh 2, Buffalo 1 (SO); Ralph Wilson Stadium, Buffalo, NY

2009: Detroit 6, Chicago 4; Wrigley Field, Chicago, IL

2010: Boston 2, Philadelphia 1 (OT); Fenway Park, Boston, MA

2011: Washington 3, Pittsburgh 1; Heinz Field, Pittsburgh, PA

2012: N.Y. Rangers 3, Philadelphia 2; Citizens Bank Park, Philadelphia, PA

2013: Not held due to NHL lockout

2014: Toronto 3, Detroit 2 (SO); Michigan Stadium, Ann Arbor, MI

2015: Washington 3, Chicago 2; Nationals Park, Washington, D.C.

2016: Montreal 5, Boston 1; Gillette Stadium, Foxboro, MA

Coolest Nicknames

Max "Dipsy Doodle Dandy" Bentley

Johnny "China Wall" Bower

Frank "Mr. Zero" Brimsek

Pavel "The Russian Rocket" Bure

Steve Buzinski, "The Puck Goesinski"

Bill "Big Whistle" Chadwick

Yvan "The Roadrunner" Cournoyer

Shawn "The Barbarian" Cronin

Tie "The Albanian Assassin" Domi

Lou "Leapin' Louie" Fontinato

Johnny "Black Cat" Gagnon

Bernie "Boom Boom" Geoffrion

Stu "The Grim Reaper" Grimson

Glenn "Mr. Goalie" Hall

Dominik "The Dominator" Hasek

Camille "The Eel" Henry

Mel "Sudden Death" Hill

Larry "Suitcase" Hillman

Gordie "Mr. Hockey" Howe

Bobby "The Golden Jet" Hull

Ed "Jovo-Cop" Jovanovski

Bob "Hound Dog" Kelly

J. Bob "Battleship" Kelly

Nikolai "The Bulin Wall" Khabibulin

Jerry "King Kong" Korab

"Terrible" Ted Lindsay

Harry "Apple Cheeks" Lumley

Chris "Knuckles" Nilan

Didier "Cannonball" Pitre

Jacques "Jake the Snake" Plante

Andre "Red Light" Racicot

Henri "Pocket Rocket" Richard

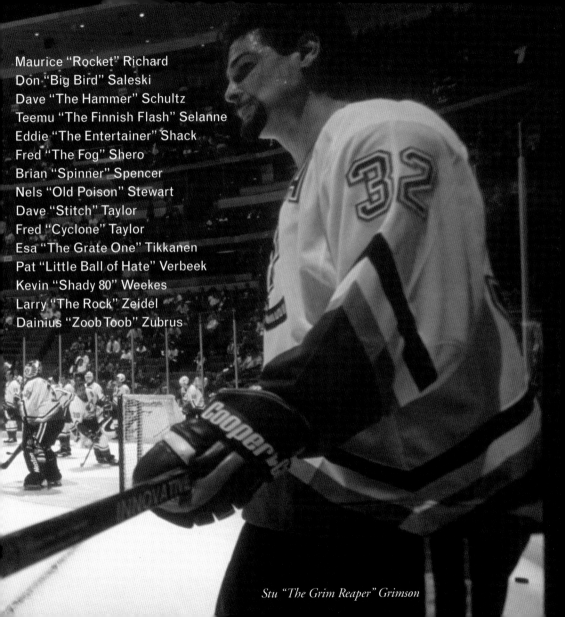

Maurice "Rocket" Richard
Don "Big Bird" Saleski
Dave "The Hammer" Schultz
Teemu "The Finnish Flash" Selanne
Eddie "The Entertainer" Shack
Fred "The Fog" Shero
Brian "Spinner" Spencer
Nels "Old Poison" Stewart
Dave "Stitch" Taylor
Fred "Cyclone" Taylor
Esa "The Grate One" Tikkanen
Pat "Little Ball of Hate" Verbeek
Kevin "Shady 80" Weekes
Larry "The Rock" Zeidel
Dainius "Zoob Toob" Zubrus

Stu "The Grim Reaper" Grimson

A League of Their Own

Hockey is not just a sport for the boys. Women have been lacing up the skates for almost as long as the game has been played on frozen lakes and ponds. In fact, women's hockey has been growing in popularity in recent decades at the college and high school levels.

In 2015–16, the professional National Women's Hockey League debuted with four teams — the Boston Pride, Buffalo Beauts, Connecticut Whale and New York Riveters. The Pride defeated the Beauts, two games to none, in March to win the inaugural Isobel Cup, named after Lady Isobel Gathorne-Hardy, daughter of Lord Stanley.

WOMEN'S OLYMPIC HOCKEY CHAMPIONS

2014, Sochi – Canada 3, USA 2 (OT)
2010, Vancouver – Canada 2, USA 0
2006, Turin – Canada 4, Sweden 1
2002, Salt Lake City – Canada 3, USA 2
1998, Nagano – USA 3, Canada 1

17-Minute Jet Flight

Fans in Winnipeg, Manitoba mourned the loss of their Jets to Phoenix (where they became the Coyotes) back in 1996, as their WHA-turned-NHL franchise relocated. Fifteen years later, they were not about to mourn again. When the Atlanta Thrashers were eyeing Manitoba as their new home in 2011, Winnipeg needed to show a strong show of support. The NHL-issued challenge: sell 13,000 season tickets in advance.

About 2,000 Manitoba Moose season ticket-holders were given first shot at the tickets, and they purchased more than 7,000. When the remainder went on sale to the general public, they sold out in 17 minutes! "While I had no doubt the 'Drive to 13,000' would reach its destination,

the remarkable speed at which it got there certifies the fans' hunger for NHL hockey," NHL commissioner Gary Bettman said, affirming the return of the Jets for the 2011–12 season.

JETS SINCE LANDING IN WINNIPEG

2011-12	37	35	10
2012-13	24	21	3
2013-14	37	35	10
2014-15	43	26	13*
2015-16	35	39	8